CW01091608

Doing their Bit

Home Front Lapel Badges
1939-1945

JON MILLS

SABRESTORM

Designed and typeset by Philip Clucas MSIAD

British Library Cataloguing in Publication Data

A catalogue record for this book is available from the
British Library

Published by Sabrestorm Publishing, 90 Lennard Road,
Dunton Green, Sevenoaks, Kent TN13 2UX

Website: www.sabrestorm.com
Email: books@sabrestorm.com

ISBN 978-0-9552723-9-4

Contents

Foreword to the Second Edition

The First Edition of this book, all 250 copies, was published privately in 1996. The badges were professionally photographed but the final result was achieved though hours on the computer, photocopier and spiral binding machine with subsequent chaos at home as the copies were assembled by hand in the kitchen. Much to my surprise the book seems to have become the standard work on the subject. The few second hand copies which turn up sell quickly and for surprising amounts of money.

I was therefore surprised but delighted when Ian Bayley of Sabrestorm asked me to produce a second edition. My original intention was to add a supplement recording badges not in the First Edition with additional information and corrections. Finding such new material presented me with a problem; although I had continued to record Home Front badges – a much simpler task since the advent of the internet and ebay where they are regularly sold - I had, apart from odd items here and there, stopped collecting them. Fellow enthusiasts Roger Miles and Steve Taylor came to my aid and I must thank them for allowing me to cause havoc in their collections. The badges I found were subsequently superbly photographed by Lauren McLean.

A chance encounter with Tim Fattorini provided an opportunity to extend the scope of the book. Tim introduced me to his cousin Tom Fattorini, of Thomas Fattorini Ltd in Birmingham, probably the largest manufacturer of wartime enamel badges. Tom was generous with his time and kindly allowed me to borrow some 200 badges which his grandfather Wilfred collected as they were manufactured. Steve Taylor photographed these as well as some badges from his own collection. Copies of Thomas Fattorini's wartime marketing literature were kindly provided by Frank Setchfield, founder of the Badge Collectors' Circle whose website at www.badgecollectorscircle.co.uk is recommended for those with an interest in all types of pin-back badges. *Grace's Guide: The Best of British Engineering 1750-1960s* proved invaluable in identifying companies which issued industrial ARP badges, especially as their website www.gracesguide.co.uk includes contemporary marketing material and advertisements.

This new material allowed me to start the new edition by looking at the wartime output of Thomas Fattorini Ltd. It then reproduces the text and illustration of the First Edition but with the supporting documents now in colour. The final section, arranged in the same order as the main text, details badges traced since 1995 with supplementary information and a few corrections. The new badge numbers continue on from the sequence in the First Edition. For clarity the images are larger than the original items by approximately 50%.

You would not be reading this without Ian Bayley suggesting an update and his invaluable enthusiasm, support and hard work in producing it. My thanks go to him and his team for such an impressive job. I could not have produced this book without the support and forbearance of my wife Lyn during the time I was writing and researching it – both now and in 1995!

I can be contacted via the publishers if anyone can provide further information on these badges, their use and manufacture.

Jon Mills

Thomas Fattorini

'Brilliant enamel badges of good design and beautiful finish'

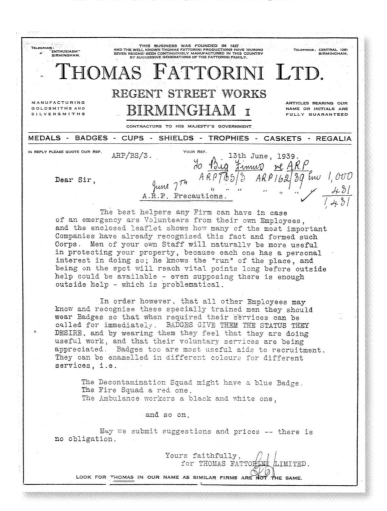

TELEGRAMS: "ENTHUSIASM" BIRMINGHAM.

THIS BUSINESS WAS FOUNDED IN 1827 AND THE WELL KNOWN THOMAS FATTORINI PRODUCTIONS HAVE (DURING SEVEN REIGNS) BEEN CONTINUOUSLY MANUFACTURED IN THIS COUNTRY BY SUCCESSIVE GENERATIONS OF THE FATTORINI FAMILY.

TELEPHONE: CENTRAL 1261 BIRMINGHAM.

THOMAS FATTORINI LTD.

REGENT STREET WORKS
BIRMINGHAM 1

MANUFACTURING GOLDSMITHS AND SILVERSMITHS

ARTICLES BEARING OUR NAME OR INITIALS ARE FULLY GUARANTEED

CONTRACTORS TO HIS MAJESTY'S GOVERNMENT

MEDALS · BADGES · CUPS · SHIELDS · TROPHIES · CASKETS · REGALIA

IN REPLY PLEASE QUOTE OUR REF. ARP/BS/3.   YOUR REF.   13th June, 1939.

Dear Sir,

A.R.P. Precautions.

> The best helpers any Firm can have in case of an emergency are Volunteers from their own Employees, and the enclosed leaflet shows how many of the most important Companies have already recognised this fact and formed such Corps. Men of your own Staff will naturally be more useful in protecting your property, because each one has a personal interest in doing so; he knows the "run" of the place, and being on the spot will reach vital points long before outside help could be available - even supposing there is enough outside help - which is problematical.

> In order however, that all other Employees may know and recognise these specially trained men they should wear Badges so that when required their services can be called for immediately. BADGES GIVE THEM THE STATUS THEY DESIRE, and by wearing them they feel that they are doing useful work, and that their voluntary services are being appreciated. Badges too are most useful aids to recruitment. They can be enamelled in different colours for different services, i.e.

> The Decontamination Squad might have a blue Badge.
> The Fire Squad a red one.
> The Ambulance workers a black and white one,

>   and so on.

> May we submit suggestions and prices -- there is no obligation.

Yours faithfully,
for THOMAS FATTORINI LIMITED.

LOOK FOR THOMAS IN OUR NAME AS SIMILAR FIRMS ARE NOT THE SAME.

It pays to deal direct with the Makers !

THOMAS FATTORINI LIMITED

REGENT STREET WORKS ○ BIRMINGHAM 1

Directors: Thomas Fattorini, Frank Fattorini, Wilfred Fattorini

'Brilliant enamel badges....'

Whilst research for the First Edition concentrated on the design and history of Home Front badges, it was noticeable that a large number of them carried on their reverse the maker's mark of Thomas Fattorini, Regent Street, Birmingham. The book would have been much thinner without their prodigious wartime output.

Antonio Fattorini arrived in England from Italy in 1827 and settled in Leeds. By the 1830s he was advertising as 'Fattorini and Sons, Goldsmiths; Skipton, Harrogate and Bradford'. Antonio's grandson added his name to the Skipton business in the 1890s when the firm became known as Thomas Fattorini. Thomas remained in charge until his death in 1934, opening several further shops and businesses. From April 1893 the gold and silver products made for his jewellery business were hallmarked at the Birmingham Assay Office and in 1919 a manufacturing business for medals and trophies was set up in the city. When day to day control of the business passed to his sons in 1928, the company became Thomas Fattorini Ltd based at Regent Street Works, Birmingham. As other branches of the family still traded under the Fattorini name all advertising material for the Birmingham business underlined Thomas and carried the slogan 'Note the Thomas in our name, similar firms are not the same'.

By the 1930s Thomas Fattorini's products in precious metals, enamels or celluloid catered 'for every conceivable purpose.' Local councils bought civic maces and chains of office for their Mayors and presented freedom scrolls to prominent citizens in Thomas Fattorini caskets. Churchgoers placed offerings on their collection plates, took communion from their communion sets and wore their badges to show that they had been or were pilgrims to destinations such as Lourdes. Clubs and associations for indoor games, motorcycling, athletics, golf, tennis, badminton and swimming awarded their cups and medals to members who wore the club's badge made by Thomas Fattorini. Trade unionists, hospital workers and those collecting for worthy causes wore their badges as did younger readers

CHILDREN'S CORNER BADGES

Get the children interested in your paper whilst they are young.
You will then have readers for life.

Have Badges which will do credit to your paper—Ask Thomas Fattorini Ltd. for a design and quotation.

Every child likes to belong to a Society and possess its Badge. This is why Children's Corners in Newspapers and Weekly Periodicals are so popular. One child has a Badge and shows it to its playmate who immediately wants one. If sent to subscribers or in return for coupons see how your circulation increases. Badges do increase circulation.

Most of our National Daily Newspapers and Weekly Journals have a Children's Corner and use Badges.

THOMAS FATTORINI LTD. REGENT STREET WORKS BIRMINGHAM, 1

BADGES for SPORTS CLUBS

Most of our National Sports Clubs have their own exclusive Badge, of which they are rightly proud. Members like to wear such Badges without which they feel "lost" almost as an outsider.

Let us design a special Badge for YOUR Club and you will be surprised at the extra keenness and enthusiasm it will create. There is no obligation in asking for designs and estimates.

THOMAS FATTORINI LTD. REGENT STREET WORKS BIRMINGHAM, 1

BADGES for HOSPITAL USE

Most Hospitals use Badges for presenting to Nurses who complete their training and Thomas Fattorini has had the pleasure and privilege of designing and making them for many important Hospitals. These Badges are always well made and consequently always popular.

A really well-known Badge—made by Thomas Fattorini Ltd.

Many famous Hospitals buy their Badges from Thomas Fattorini Ltd., Regent Street, Works, Birmingham, 1.

BADGES FOR RAISING FUNDS.
Enormous profits have been made for Hospitals from the use of Badges. Ask us for further details.

THOMAS FATTORINI LTD. REGENT STREET WORKS BIRMINGHAM, 1

ADVERTISING BADGES

Most of our large National Advertisers use Badges and the repeat orders we get prove their worth as useful advertising.

A nice Badge costing a few pence will be worn and seen for a very long time after all other kinds of advertisement are forgotten.

The cost of Badges is negligible compared with the advantages.

Ask us for a quotation and special sketches — there is no obligation.

THOMAS FATTORINI LTD. REGENT STREET WORKS BIRMINGHAM, 1

of newspapers; those joining the *Daily Mail's* Teddy Tail Club received a Thomas Fattorini badge for, as their advertising stressed, 'Get the children interested in your paper whilst they are young. You will then have readers for life.' If you attended a conference or trade exhibition between the wars the delegates or salesmen were 'quickly and easily identified by prospective customers' by their Thomas Fattorini badges. Salesmen were likely to send you on your way with a celluloid advertising badge for your children or a mirror-backed one for your wife. Celluloid badges at five guineas a thousand and elaborate silver cups at six pounds each were amongst the extensive range of souvenirs offered to commemorate the Coronation in May 1937.

The creation of the Air Raid Precautions services and the compulsory extension of ARP measures to major employers by the Civil Defence Act of 1939 opened up a new market. In June 1939 1,400 of Britain's largest companies received Thomas Fattorini's leaflet and

letter suggesting that to help employees know and recognise specially trained ARP staff 'they should wear badges so that when required their services can be called upon immediately.' Such badges, they suggested, gave volunteers status and showed appreciation of their services. As the examples show many companies took their advice and ordered badges enamelled in different colours to indicate the separate services. The next few pages record just a small sample of Thomas Fattorini's wartime output, all of which provide proof that to purchase the company's products was to 'Buy Badges which are Works of Art'.

DOING THEIR BIT....

Industrial ARP badges manufactured by Thomas Fattorini Ltd

TF1

TF2

TF3

TF4

TF5

TF6

TF7

TF8

TF9

TF10

TF11

TF12

TF13

TF14

TF15

TF16

TF17

TF18

TF19

TF20

TF21

TF22

TF23

TF24

TF25

TF26

TF27

TF28

TF29

TF30

TF31

TF32

TF33

TF34

TF35

TF36

VARIATIONS ON A THEME BY THOMAS FATTORINI

The First Edition shows badge C13 used by the ARP teams of Express Dairies.
The same design was widely copied

TF37

TF38

TF39

TF40

TF41

TF42

TF43

TF44

TF45

TF46

TF47

TF48

TF49

TF50

TF51

TF52

TF53

TF54

TF55

ARP BADGES FROM UNIDENTIFIED COMPANIES

Thomas Fattorini no longer have records of the wartime badges they manufactured.
Are the companies that ordered these badges ever likely be identified?

TF56   TF57   TF58

TF59   TF60   TF61

TF62   TF63   TF64

TF65

TF66

TF67

TF68

TF69

TF70

TF71

TF72

TF73

TF74   TF75

Introduction

The lapel or pin back-badge is perhaps the most commonly encountered souvenir of the civilian war effort in the United Kingdom between 1939 and 1945. Primarily because of its size, it has been stored as a treasured memento in many a chest of drawers or needlework box, to be rediscovered years later, often by someone to whom its significance and meaning are unknown. Whilst badges that have a military origin have been exhaustively catalogued, no published attempt has yet been made to identify these Home Front items. In the absence of a uniform these were often the only sign of membership that some people, whose wartime efforts were significant, possessed. This book is an attempt to identify the most commonly encountered types of these badges.

It was for many organisations the lack of a uniform that stimulated the use of these badges in the first place. Initially these war-related insignia were issued to members of organisations who, during their spare time, were training for a role in any future war. The aim was to distinguish these volunteers from their fellow citizens and thereby raise the profile of the organisations to which they belonged. The Air Raid Precautions (ARP) badge and those for the reserve forces such as the Territorial Army (TA) and Royal Air Force Volunteer Reserve (RAFVR) are examples of these. Conditions of issue varied - whilst the ARP services stipulated that those to whom the badge was issued should reach a certain standard of training before acquiring it, the reserve forces issued it to all members on enlistment. In a similar category come badges issued to members of industrial ARP services. Here, again in the absence of some sort of uniform, they served not only as signs to encourage others, but also as identifying marks in an emergency at work.

As the war progressed other badges appeared, either to indicate membership of an organisation when out of uniform, or as the sole identifying mark when no uniform was issued. After 1942, as supplies of almost everything became scarce, many organisations had to make do with a lapel badge in the absence of a desired uniform.

A further category of badge is that indicating support for, or work with a particular cause. These range from those of the pre-war national organisations such as the Red Cross and St John's Ambulance, through to those working for or supporting organisations such as the Association of French Volunteers. Fund-raising badges from the period are scarce. This is in part due to the lack of materials, including metal, paper and pins, but also to the severely restricted fund-raising carried out in this way during the war years. The traditional paper flag on a pin is outside the scope of this book, but the tin badge with a paper and celluloid cover is included where its use was widespread.

Badges from the period come in a variety of materials. The earliest ones were metal, often precious metal such as silver. This is the case with the ARP badge and those issued to the reserve forces and is of interest as it allows badges to be dated from the hallmark. Enamelled badges are frequently encountered: the resources which went into keeping in production these highly coloured symbols must have been immense and something of a drain on the country's labour and materials.

From 1942 onwards, as materials of all sorts got scarce, so too did new badges. Metal-saving "austerity" badges were made in an early plastic material as used for army cap badges or even of paper and card, sometimes with a textured surface resembling leather. Tin badges, of the type still familiar today, were never as widely used for lapel badges as more solid metal types, possibly because of their fragile nature. Mainly restricted to fund-raising events, they do occasionally appear as identifying marks for CD services.

Where inscriptions on badges are described they appear as written, with oblique strokes indicating breaks in lines or scrolls (e.g. Red/Penny-A-Week Fund/Cross). Fixings on badges are of three types. Those with a horseshoe shaped or stud lapel fixing were designed for wear in the lapels of a man's suit. Those with pin backs were usually designed for wear by women, but this is not a hard and fast rule. Many badges with pin fastenings were clearly designed to be fixed to overalls.

Some badges which look like and are collected as, lapel badges are in fact no such thing. Examples of some of the more commonly confused types are included, with an indication of their true purpose. Some can legitimately be included in collections of both lapel badges and other insignia such as cap badges, having been used as both. Examples would include the badge of ENSA in bronze or the WVS badge, originally designed as a qualification badge and later worn as a cap or beret badge by the service.

To put these badges into context, each section includes, where details are available, a short history of the organisation wearing the badge, its wartime role and the number of members or badge wearers. If it has been possible to establish a date when a badge was approved, introduced or manufactured this has also been included. Many organisations issued some form of authorisation to wear their badge or some form of identification for badge wearers. Examples of some of these are illustrated in the text, together with other documentary evidence of the organisation.

This book aims to identify and place in their historical context some of the more regularly encountered badges of the period. No book like this could every hope to be comprehensive, nor completely certain about all its facts. In some cases identification is tentative or the date of use uncertain. Where the explanation of an item is conjectural this is indicated. The author would be glad to have further information on any of these items or illustrations of any badges not mentioned in these pages, or to hear from anyone who can add details on any of the organisations mentioned.

Although the majority of the items illustrated are from the author's collection, it would have been impossible to complete such a book without the help of many friends and fellow collectors. My thanks to John Ingham, Geoffrey Poulter, Chris Young but especially the ever-patient Roy Goodey for the loan of some of the badges illustrated. My thanks also to Godfrey New for his excellent photography, and Trevor Kingsley-Curry for establishing just what a hard job the photography would be. My especial thanks to Lyn, who has cheerfully supported me throughout the enormous amount of time it takes to complete a project such as this.

Jon Mills
September 1996

RAIDS
OR
NO
RAIDS

Twice a Citizen

The Reserve Forces

The Reserve Forces

Prior to the creation of the ARP services in the mid-1930s, the usual way for volunteers to serve their country in time of peace was to join one of the reserve forces. Both the Army and the Navy had reserves established in the nineteenth century, whilst the RAF, itself only created in 1918, had established its own reserve in the 1920s.

The Army's reserve, the **Territorial Army (TA)**, could trace its origins back to the 1850s, but it had been re-established with this title after the First World War. Members were civilian volunteers trained in local units representing all the arms and services of the Army with a liability for full-time service on the declaration of war. Their role became more important and more visible after 1935 when the TA became responsible for the anti-aircraft defences of the entire United Kingdom.

In the inter-war period, the county Territorial Army and Auxiliary Air Force Associations (TAAFAs) who administered local units, had pressed the War Office for some tangible recognition of the services of TA volunteers. It was suggested that this might take the form either of a certificate to be hung at home, or a badge to be worn in civilian clothes. By 1935 the preference of most Associations was for a badge. In March 1937 the War Office finally agreed that, following the example of the ARP badge announced the previous month, (see page 34), the TA would also have a badge.

White metal was chosen in preference to the bronze colour suggested by some, as it was seen as a tangible link with the white metal insignia worn on the uniforms of the pre-1908 Volunteer Force. Designs were commissioned from a commercial designer, George Kruger Gray, but these were eventually discarded in favour of one from a Mr Coombes of the Royal Mint. Following War Office agreement to the design in December 1937, the badge was approved by the King in March 1938. An initial order for 250,000 badges was placed with the Mint on 19th March.

The badge **(A1)** consists of the letters "TA" between two horizontal lines across the centre of a circle. Below the circle is a lion springing aggressively forward with legs outstretched, the whole being surmounted by a crown. Badges were of sterling silver with a lapel fixing in base metal, a number being stamped into the fixing.

Badges Numbers One and Two were presented to the King and Queen as Honorary Colonels of TA regiments. The design was also used extensively on recruiting literature for the TA in the period 1938 to 1939 and, with a Queen's crown, is still used today

It was announced in Parliament in March 1938 that the badge was to be issued to all TA officers and other ranks on enlistment, a certificate accompanying each badge as a form of authorisation. Following the decision at the beginning of 1939 to double the size of the TA, a further 275,000 badges were ordered from the Mint. Issue of the badge ceased in September 1939 when the TA became an integral part of the army.

All the original badges had a lapel fixing, but on the revival of the TA in 1947, a further supply of badges was made with a pin and brooch fitting for issue to female members of the **Auxiliary Territorial Service (ATS)**, later **Women's Royal Army Corps (WRAC)**. These badges were made by Gaunt using the Royal Mint's original dies. The ATS had been formed in July 1938 as a female equivalent of the TA and had included companies for service with the RAF. On the outbreak of war the ATS become the only women's army corps. Illustrated **(A2)** is a numbered lapel badge, similar in design to the cap badge of the service, which looks to be an equivalent of the TA badge but for which no issue details have yet come to light. The fact that it is numbered suggests that it is an official issue.

Following the creation of the TA badge for those in established units, the War Office came back to the Mint in June 1939 with a request for lapel badges for those ex-servicemen who, having completed their full-time service, retained an individual liability for further service in the reserves. For other ranks there was the **Royal Army Reserve (RAR), (A3)** originally simply the Army Reserve but renamed in June 1938. Officers formed the **Regular Army Reserve of Officers (RARO) (A4)**. In addition there was a third reserve the **Army Officers Emergency Reserve (OER)** which consisted of men between the ages of 31 and 55 who felt that they might be eligible for commissioned service in time of war. A badge for this third body was requested in July 1939, but does not appear to have been manufactured. These badges were not finally produced by the Mint, but the existence of the RARO badge was announced in the national press in July 1939.

The design for both badges was similar, being based around the Army crest introduced in May 1938. The crest, comprising crossed swords surmounted by a crown and lion, had originally been created for use in a memorial window at Ypres cathedral in 1935, but had been simplified for other uses by the Army as a whole. On the lapel badges it formed the central device and was surrounded by a circlet on which appeared the appropriate Reserve's title, the whole surmounted by a crown. The badges are sterling and hallmarked.

The Air Force, the youngest of the three services, had created an equivalent of the TA the **Auxiliary Air Force (AAF)**, in 1924. Administered by the local TAAFAs, units were raised as numbered air force squadrons with strong ties to their local areas. Twenty AAF flying squadrons existed in 1939 as well as fifty-four squadrons created since May 1938 to man the anti-aircraft balloon defences of the UK. In July 1936, the RAF announced the creation of a further reserve, the **RAF Volunteer Reserve (RAFVR)**, designed to train individuals as pilots outside the AAF squadrons, through a network of local flying schools run by civilian contractors.

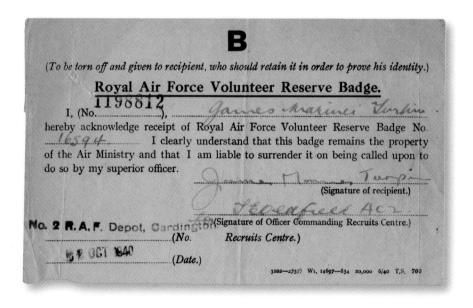

Following the example of the War Office, the Air Ministry approached the Mint in October 1938 to request badges along the lines of the TA badge for their two reserves. The design **(A5)** closely follows that of the TA but the central device is the RAF eagle and initials of the reserve. After approval by the King in April 1939, production of 25,000 AAF and 30,000

RAFVR badges was ordered, deliveries commencing in June 1939. On the outbreak of war recruiting for the AAF was suspended, all recruits to the RAF for the duration of the war being channelled through the RAFVR. Many of those eventually called up had the beginning of their active service deferred for some time after their initial recruitment but were issued with an RAFVR lapel badge to signify their enlistment. For this reason, supplies of the badges continued to be obtained from the Mint until 1944, the numbering sequence rising into the 900,000s. A certificate accompanied each badge

At the end of June 1939, the Royal Air Force companies created within the ATS were separated to form a **Women's Auxiliary Air Force (WAAF)**. On 5th August the Air Ministry asked the Mint to create a lapel for this new force by adding the letter W to the front of the initials on the existing AAF badge, but plans for production of this were shelved in November 1939.

The RAFVR badge was re-introduced in 1947 for the revived Reserve. As with the TA badge, stocks were at this time manufactured with a pin brooch fitting for issue to members of the **Women's Royal Air Force Reserve**. Several brass and enamel versions of the RAFVR badge exist **(A6,A7)** which are probably post-war private purchase versions designed to look more spectacular than the plain white metal version.

The Royal Navy also created two main reserves: the **Royal Naval Reserve (RNR)** in the nineteenth century from men who were employed as seamen in civilian life and the **Royal Naval Volunteer Reserve (RNVR)** in 1903 from those interested in the sea but not earning a living from it. As far as is known, no lapel badge for civilian clothes was issued by either of these two reserves.

A lapel does however exist for one small section of the naval reserves. In 1932, bowing to pressure from the many enthusiasts for the new art of wireless operation anxious to bring their skills to the national service if required, the Admiralty created the **Royal Naval Wireless Auxiliary Reserve (RNWAR)**. Members, aged between 18 and 45, were either already amateur radio operators or enthusiasts with an interest in wireless telegraphy. Although there was no legal basis for this reserve, volunteers were trained to act as telegraphists for service with the Royal Navy. They received no uniform but were asked to hold themselves ready to be mobilised in time of war. The position of this reserve was regularised in January 1939 when the RNWAR became the Wireless Section of the RNVR and, together with specialists from the Royal Fleet Reserve and naval pensioners formed the **Royal Naval Volunteer (Wireless) Reserve (RNVWR)**. In common with all reserve forces the RNVWR was mobilised in 1939 becoming an integral part of the Royal Navy. The RNVWR was reconstituted in 1947, losing its separate identity in 1957 on the reorganisation of the naval reserves which resulted in the disappearance of the Royal Naval Volunteer Reserve.

Two lapels are known, one from each phase of the reserve's pre-war existence **(A8, A9)**. They are unusual for reservists in being made in coloured enamels, a distinction which may be related to the lack of a uniform in the early years. The design features the lightning flash and wings of the naval telegraphist's qualification badge rendered in gold on blue. Around the lower part is a crescent shape in white on which appear the letters of the appropriate reserve in gold. The whole is surmounted by a crown.

A1

A2

A3

A4

A5

A6

A7

A8

A9

We must be Prepared

ARP and Civil Defence

ARP and Civil Defence

From the mid-nineteen twenties the Government became increasingly aware that in any future war, a major threat to Britain's civilian population would come from enemy aircraft dropping bombs to start fires, cause explosions or spread poison gas. To combat these threats they created from 1935 a series of new civilian volunteer services controlled by the local government authorities. These volunteers manned first-aid posts and parties, staffed report centres, drove ambulances and served in the front line of attack as Air Raid Wardens. The overall name for these services was **Air Raid Precautions (ARP)**. Created specifically to meet the new wartime threats, they are perhaps the most widely recognised civilian services of the period.

After completion of a course of training, volunteers received a government issue sterling silver badge **(B1)**, to acknowledge their contribution and to make the service more visible in public life. Designed by the well-known sculptor Eric Gill, this was made at the Royal Mint. With permission of the King, it incorporated in its design the Imperial Crown. Authorised in February 1937, the Metropolitan Borough of Hampstead claimed to issue the first badges in London in December of the same year. Original issues were hallmarked, but from 1940 they were made in white metal by commercial manufacturers. Many badges were numbered by the issuing authorities, but the example shown **(B2)** is unusual in having the number stamped on the face rather than the reverse. As early as February 1939 nearly 801,000 badges had been delivered to local authorities.

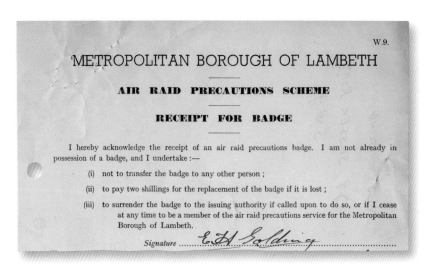

From 1941 the badge was authorised as a cap badge. Manufacture ceased in 1943, by which time most volunteers wore uniform and there was no need for a lapel badge. Two types were issued, each with a distinctive coloured box to identify the type of fixing and thus make easier the job of those issuing them. A badge with a stud fixing for men came in a red box whilst a blue box contained a pin back badge for women. Almost as soon as they were issued, wearers began to complain that the badge was too large and commercial manufacturers were quick to seize on this as the pretext for producing smaller versions often with enamel colouring absent from the original. Two examples of these **(B3,B4)** are illustrated.

Following the announcement of the ARP badge, the Governor of Malta wrote to the Colonial Office requesting permission to adopt the badge for the island's ARP services, with the addition of "Malta" below the design. Having sought the approval of the Home Office and the permission of the King to use the crown, the Colonial Office wrote to the Governors of all Colonies and Dependent Territories in December 1937 informing them that permission had been granted for the badge (as long as it was not worn in the United Kingdom) and instructing them to submit requests through the Crown Agents for the Colonies. A decision was made in August 1938 that all overseas badges would be fitted with a pin rather than a lapel fixing, this being more suitable for tropical clothing and that the pin should be shortened to avoid the danger of the wearer pricking himself because of the thinner materials.

No complete list of these badges seems to have survived but examples are known for Hong Kong **(B5)**, Gibraltar, Kenya, and the Straits Settlements, which includes Singapore, the last of these being hallmarked from Birmingham in 1938.

To emphasise their independence, many local authorities had made at their own expense a bewildering variety of lapel and pin back badges, many of which went on being worn long after the arrival of the official badge. Typical is that from **Gravesend** in Essex **(B6)** incorporating the local arms and the abbreviation ARP. Others used their crest with the words "Air Raid Precautions" in full , such as the example from **Aylesbury (B7)**. Subsequent to the issue of the national badge, features from it were incorporated into local badges. The designs from **Chesterfield (B8)** and **Doncaster (B9)** are examples.

Several local authorities, eager to generate a sense of *esprit de corps* in these new organisations, set individual services up with separate badges. Wardens, always the largest of the services, produced several badges. Members of the The **Cheshire Corps of Air Raid Wardens (B10)** and the **City of Salford Air Raid Wardens Corps (B11)** both benefited from distinctive badges, whilst Northampton went one stage further, issuing a separate design for its **Women's Wardens Service (B12)**. Brighton issued a separate badge for what is believed to be its **Chemical Warfare Defence Service (B13)**, whilst the **Messenger Organisations** in **Manchester (B14)** and **Worcester**

(B15) both wore the badges shown, the former incorporating the City's Busy Bee symbol. All of these services quickly developed their own rank structure and some badge designs such as that from **Birmingham (B16)**, incorporated the wearer's rank as well.

From the outset, those qualified as instructors in ARP felt that they merited a mark of their accomplishment. For several years the government resisted all requests for a separate badge, feeling that the general ARP badge was sufficient for the trained worker at all levels. In the absence of a national badge, local authorities simply produced their own. Examples from **Bedfordshire (B17)** and **Liverpool (B18)** are shown. **Midland ARP Region** set up an instructors' association which produced yet another badge **(B19)**. In January 1942 however, in response to the repeated requests, a government approved instructor's badge was finally issued. Four classes of instructor were recognised, two trained on national courses and two trained locally. The design for all classes consisted of a red enamel upright oval crossed by a bar bearing the word "Instructor", the whole surmounted by the crown. On the lower half of the oval appeared the words "Civil Defence", on the upper part the designation of the level of qualification. For **Instructors, Air Raid Precautions School (ARPS) (B20)** and **Instructors, Civil Anti-Gas School (CAGS)**, that is those who had qualified on national courses, the background of the badge was gold coloured. For **Instructors, Local Air Raid Precautions (LARP) (B21)** and **Instructors, Local Anti-Gas Course (LAGC) (B22)** the background colour was silver. A further badge of this type for which no issue details have been found was worn by Rescue Service Instructors. This is the same shape as the badges noted above with the word "Instructor" across the central bar. Around the oval appear the words "CD" and "Rescue" in gold on dark green, the whole surmounted by a crown.

This national instructor's badge was recognised by authorities but was considered neither a service badge nor an essential mark of qualification. Those qualified to wear it were required to purchase their own from the local authority, although some authorities met the cost and issued them free. If worn in uniform, regulations stated that the badge was to be pinned through the flap of the left collar or, if the collar was worn closed, to the left breast. There are numerous illustrations to show that this instruction was disregarded. Alternative fixings of pin or stud type were available. Policemen qualified as ARP instructors (in many areas Wardens were under the direct control of the police) were specifically prohibited from wearing the badge in uniform, but could wear it with civilian clothes.

In 1941 the ARP Services were renamed **Civil Defence General Services** to indicate more accurately their enlarged role. No new government badge was approved, as by this time most volunteers wore uniform. Commercial badge manufacturers however revised their designs to reflect the new title. In some the shape was altered slightly, the tablet becoming completely oval, the letters "CD" appearing in the centre in silver on blue, all surmounted by a crown. This design **(B23)** followed closely that used on Home Guard lapels (see N1) and was possibly done to economise in the use of moulds. One variation **(B24)** had, attached below the main badge, five inverted red bars representing the service chevrons introduced for wear on uniforms in February 1944. Other designs **(B25, B26)** reflected the device worn on the Civil Defence armlet introduced in July 1940, with the words "Civil Defence" and semi-circular lines in an arc.

Two further badges show the contrasts encountered in these lapels. The more elaborate badge **(B27)**, originating in London, incorporates the Borough's arms in the centre and the designation "**Civil Defence Bethnal Green**" around the edge. At the opposite end of the design scale is the tin badge **(B28)** from the **Caterham and Warlingham Urban District Council** in Surrey, the lettering "ARPV" standing for Air Raid Precautions Volunteer.

Before the outbreak of war, many felt that there was insufficient support for the development of these services. Consequently in February 1939 there was established the **Air Raid Defence League**, "to secure effective air raid protection as a primary object of national policy". The League described itself as wishing to occupy, in relation to air raid precautions, a position similar to that of the Air and Navy Leagues (see pages 210 & 222). Membership was open to all interested in the subject, an annual subscription of 1/- (5p) being payable. Initially affiliated to, and eventually incorporated with the League was the newly-formed **National Association of Air Raid Wardens**. The League had two designs of lapel badge. The first **(B29)** incorporates at its centre the Union flag with the title around the edge, but subsequent to the incorporation of the Wardens' Association, the centre was changed to include the initials "ARW" for Air Raid Warden **(B30)**. The League faded from public prominence once the war began, as by that time few local authorities needed reminding of the vital role played by these new services.

B

B1

B2

B3

B4

B5

B6

B7

B8

B9

B10

B11

B12

B13

B14

B15

B16

B17

B18

We must be Prepared

B19

B20

B21

B22

B23

B24

B25

B26

B27

B28   B29   B30

The Box for a Man's Badge

The Box for a Lady's Badge

Production must be maintained

Industrial ARP

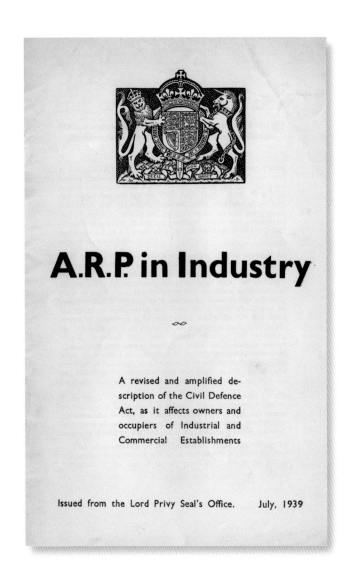

Industrial ARP

The ARP services established from 1935 concerned themselves with the protection of the general public - the man or woman in the street or in their homes. Separate arrangements were required when the citizen was at work. The Civil Defence Act, introduced in July 1939, made it a statutory duty for employers with over fifty staff to organise ARP services in their firms or factories and to train a certain percentage of their employees in ARP duties. Many forward-thinking employers had established such services after publication of the earlier ARP Act in 1937, but they had done so voluntarily. The Times newspaper in London for example had, by July 1938, already recruited 120 staff to its ARP service and divided them into three branches. The 1939 Act recommended that approximately ten per cent of a firm's staff should be enlisted for ARP duties. They were to be divided into branches similar to those in the local authority ARP services - wardens, fire services, first aid personnel and anti-gas decontamination staff.

Almost immediately the need to identify members of ARP services to their fellow workers spawned the lapel badge. It is impossible to estimate how many of these industrial ARP badges exist or even to compile a comprehensive list of companies which issued them, but in June 1940, the Home Secretary informed Parliament that industry had already recruited about 150,000 men and women to its ARP services. These industrial ARP badges record many long-vanished British companies and industries and for that reason alone deserve some form of recognition. If not already obvious from the design, the badges have, where possible, been identified with their firms.

The most regularly encountered forms of badge incorporate the company's name, initials or logo joined with the letters "ARP". Whilst those with company names in full can be associated with specific companies, **(C1 to C13)**, those which simply feature initials or a logo **(C14 to C27)** can be extremely hard to associate with the issuing company, unless like those from the **General Electric Company** (GEC) **(C14)** and **British Petroleum (C15)** the company is better known, even today, by its initials. In at least one recorded instance (not illustrated), the letters "PAD", standing for Passive Air Defence, the title more usually used by the armed forces for these services, are used instead of ARP.

In some cases this simple theme is supplemented by a device to identify individual services; for example, different coloured enamels applied to badges to differentiate each service, as with those from the **Fairey Aviation Company (C28 to C31)** and **Times Newspaper (C32, C33)**.

To make sure these colours were understood, details were often printed on documents such as security passes. In other companies an area on the badge bore the service title or an additional bar or scroll with the service name was attached : - this is shown in the Wardens' badges from **J & G Wells Collieries (C34)**, **John Bright & Brothers (C35)** and **BFS Co. Ltd (C36)** and on the specialist service badges from the London-based

THE 600 GROUP OF COMPANIES

GEORGE COHEN, SONS & COMPANY LTD. ★ K & L STEELFOUNDERS AND ENGINEERS LTD. ★ T. C. JONES & COMPANY LTD. ★ BROWETT LINDLEY LTD. ★ METALCLAD LTD. ★ THE SELSON MACHINE TOOL COMPANY LTD. ★ THE NEW LONDON ELECTRON WORKS LTD. ★ POLLOCK, BROWN & COMPANY LTD. ★ WESTBOURNE PARK COAL AND IRON COMPANY LTD. ★ SOUTHALL & HAYES COAL AND IRON COMPANY LTD.

A Statement of PRODUCTION FOR WAR

The following data of our Companies' War Effort are by no means exhaustive since lack of space prevents comprehensible description of many of our Manufactures and Products — but the quantities and particulars cited may not seem unworthy of record:—

★ Manufactures :

AMMUNITION, WARLIKE STORES, etc.

AERIAL BOMBS for Filling—4,000 lb., 1,900 lb., 1,000 lb., 500 lb. and 250 lb.	490,000
Smaller Aerial Bombs	2,400,000
AERIAL BOMB COMPONENTS	Over 3,000,000
SHELL for Filling—9.2", 6", 5.5", 4.5", 95 m.m., 25 pdr., 17 pdr., 6 pdr., etc.	4,500,000
TRENCH MORTAR BOMBS for Filling—4.5" and 3"	570,000
ROCKETS—Major Components	Over 2,250,000
PARAVANES	860
FLAIL EQUIPMENT for TANKS—Developed, Manufactured and Fitted	Several Hundred Sets
BAILEY BRIDGE PANELS—Complete with Components	15,500
BRIDGING CRIBS	4,000
INGLIS BRIDGES—Complete with Launching Gear	200

AIRCRAFT WORK

NACELLES	4,000
WING DETAILS—Sets	1,250
ENGINE MOUNTINGS	Many Hundred
HYDRAULIC UNITS for Retractable Wheels	Tens of Thousands

PLANT, MACHINERY, STEEL CASTINGS, etc.

'JONES' MOBILE CRANES	1,500
'JONES' TRENCH CRANES	400
PETROL ENGINES	5,500
STEAM ENGINES & AIR COMPRESSORS, up to 5,000 cu. ft. per minute	425
STEEL CASTINGS for Tanks, Bridges, Gun Mountings, etc.	52,000 tons
FIVE COMPLETE PLANTS for ELECTRIC POWER STATIONS—Sent to Russia	

CONSTRUCTIONAL & CIVIL ENGINEERING WORK

AEROPLANE HANGARS	450
CONCRETE REINFORCING BARS	Thousands of Tons
STEEL-MESH REINFORCEMENT	Over 2,000,000 sq. yds.
MACHINE SHOPS, FOUNDRIES & OTHER INDUSTRIAL BUILDINGS— Fabricated and Erected all over the country	Many Hundred

We played a major part in the construction of REINFORCED CAISSONS for MULBERRY HARBOUR; also in the recovery and transportation of essential plant from bombed works and wharves to new sites.

★ Plant, Machinery & Industrial Equipment Supplied :

RECONDITIONED & SECONDHAND MACHINERY

Electrical Plant, Power Plant, Boilers, Colliery and Mining Plant, Sheet-Metal Machinery, Contractors' Plant, Plastic Moulding & Rubber Machinery, etc., etc.	Tens of Thousands of Machines
RAILS & STEEL SECTIONS	60,000 Tons
NEW ENGINEERS' & CONTRACTORS' TOOLS, etc.	More than a Million
NEW MACHINE TOOLS	12,800

We acted as Sole Agents to the MINISTRY OF SUPPLY (Machine Tool Control) for USED MACHINE TOOLS Our FLEET of CONTRACTORS' PLANT, comprising over 1,000 Excavators, Bulldozers, Cranes, Concrete Mixers, etc., has been kept working to capacity.

★ Raw Materials Supplied :

FERROUS SCRAP for the IRON & STEEL INDUSTRIES & NON-FERROUS SCRAP for the FOUNDRIES and ROLLING MILLS, etc.—including that resulting from the demolition and dismantling of Obsolete Industrial Plants and Structures, the Crystal Palace Towers, Gasholders, Old Guns, Limbers and Tanks, Damaged Premises, etc.	Hundreds of Thousands of Tons
TIN-COATED SCRAP and OLD TINS DETINNED	Over 100,000 Tons
TIN from DE-TINNING	Over 1,000 Tons

Production must be maintained

Projectile & Engineering Co. (C37) and the **British Oil and Cake Mills (C38)**. In the case of the badge from **R A Lister and Co. (C39)** the word "Officer" appears on the bar.

Many badges were based on that issued to those qualified for service in local authority ARP services (see Section B). Those from **George Cohen and Co. (C40)** and **The Pressed Steel Co. (C41)** are examples - and are also obviously variations on the same basic design. Similarly the badge from **Turner Brothers Asbestos Co. (C42)** incorporates the entire ARP badge, a misunderstanding of its role, as the badge was strictly intended for those trained for the local authority ARP services. In October 1939 the government agreed that the crown should appear only on a very limited number of badges issued for National Service schemes. These commercial badges must therefore either originate from before that date or, probably unwittingly, simply have been made in contravention of this rule.

It is interesting to note the badge **(C27)** produced by the **600 Group of Companies** of which George Cohen formed a part (see advertisement). Perhaps this was introduced at a later date to replace the earlier badge incorporating the ARP design.

Several employers clearly put great store on the contribution of their staff to ARP work and followed the government's lead in making their badges in hallmarked silver:- those from **Vickers Armstrong** (**C43**, hallmarked Birmingham 1938) **J & E Hall** (**C44**, made by J R Gaunt and hallmarked London 1939) and the unidentified firm, **CT & S Ltd (C45)** are typical.

Amongst the most vital services for the continuation of normal life under air raid conditions were those provided by the public utility companies, suppliers of gas, water and electricity. Lapels are illustrated for three of these, **The Castleford Gas Group (C46)**, incorporating part of the ARP badge, but without the crown, **Glasgow Corporation Gas Department (C47)**, incorporating the gas industry's character, Mr Therm, and a simple design from the **Sheffield Corporation Waterworks (C48)**.

Some ARP services in commercial concerns had a dual responsibility to both staff and customers and this was particularly true of the ARP staff belonging to retail chains. **Marks & Spencer** established its ARP service in July 1939, each store having a chief warden reporting to the store manager. Wardens **(C49)**, fire officers **(C50)**, first-aiders and storemen were also appointed each with a distinctive badge of diamond shape but with a separate colour and symbol for each service. Two versions of the fire badge from M & S are known, one with a white ground (illustrated) the other with the colours reversed

No. **943**

J. STONE & CO., LTD.—CIVIL DEFENCE SCHEME
ENROLMENT CERTIFICATE.

This is to certify that the undermentioned employee of Messrs. J. Stone & Co., Ltd., has been enrolled as a Volunteer in the Company's A.R.P. Civil Defence Organisation in the *Fire Prevention* Section and his/her name has been included in the list of Civil Defence workers lodged with the appropriate authority in accordance with the requirements of the Personal Injuries (Civilians) Scheme.

Name. *HEATH . C.*

Shop or Dept. *Progress* Check No. ....

Date of Enrolment. *1 Sept 1939.*

(Signed) *A.J.C. Williams.*
Chief Warden
J. STONE & COMPANY, LIMITED.

> **DO NOT LOSE THIS CERTIFICATE IT IS YOUR INSURANCE POLICY.**

Production must be maintained

to show a white design on red. Also illustrated are the badges from the **Royal Arsenal Co-operative Society (RACS) (C51)** whose grocery and department stores were prominent features in the High Streets of South East London, and its Midlands counterpart the **Birmingham Co-operative Society (C52)**.

Many of these badges were prime examples of 1930s art and design with a distinctive curve to fit the letters "ARP" within a circle being popular on many of them **(C4,C6,C7,C13,C32,C36,C51)**. Manufacturers did not always start from scratch with new designs and it is obvious that badges for several different companies were based on the same concept. Those for **W D & H O Wills (C12)** in Bristol and for the Wardens of **Wells Collieries (C34)** for example are clearly the same badge. Again, those for the **General Electric Company (C14)** and the unidentified company **M R (C26)** are simply the same basic badge with different initials.

The badge from **Fairfield Shipbuilding and Engineering (C53)** in Glasgow also appears without the company name and with a scroll for "Aux Fire" fixed below **(C54)**, although it is impossible to be certain whether they were produced for the same company. This badge also illustrates that many ARP services were built on existing works fire brigades, as does the badge from the unidentified **ARP Fire Brigade (C55)** the design for which incorporates a symbol used extensively in the early days of auxiliary fire brigades. Two further similar designs, possibly copied from existing badges related to education, show the extensive and all pervading nature of these industrial ARP measures, both the **Swansea Cinemas** and an unnamed **Factory Service** having essentially the same badge.

The majority of industrial ARP badges are individually numbered, probably to conform with a pass bearing the same works or plant number. Whilst in most cases these numbers appear on the reverse, usually on the lapel fixing, in some examples they are stamped into the face. The badge from **The Wallis Tin Stamping Company (C58)** however has stamped into its front the number of the ARP Shelter Trench, possibly intended for wear by the Shelter Warden in charge.

It was vital for the war effort that employees in industry continued their work, even under air raid conditions. At the beginning of the Blitz in 1940, work stopped every time the air raid warning sounded, creating enormous disruption to production. From October, companies employed **Roof Spotters** who sounded a local air raid alarm only if there was imminent danger. It would be logical to assume that these spotters were issued with lapel badges but none have yet come to light. Even with these precautions, working during air raids was not a pleasant task, a fact recognised by at least one employer. Illustrated **(C59)** is a badge from the unidentified company **TMC**, awarded for "Continuing production during air raids". Interestingly, this is a revival of a custom from the First World War, during which telephone operators of the **London Telephone Service** were issued with the badge shown **(C60)**, which is quite often confused with those of the Second War.

As mentioned earlier, some of these badges may never be identified with any degree of certainty, the final two being examples of some mysteries. The first for **KMC ARP (C61)** has at its centre the Red Cross. Officially, this is the emblem of the Red Cross Society and should only be used by them. Was some over enthusiastic designer unaware of this, or does it simply have no connection with medical work at all? The badge for the **OEC School Warden (C62)** poses another problem. All areas vulnerable to air attack were emptied of their children at the outbreak of war, although many subsequently came back. Was this fact recognised by the Education Committee (presumed to be what the initials EC stand for) and the post of school ARP warden created to ensure their safety?

C1

C2

C3

C4

C5

C6

C7

C8

C9

Production must be maintained

C10

C11

C12

C13

C14

C15

C16

C17

C18

C19

C20

C21

C22

C23

C24

C25

C26

C27

Production must be maintained

C28

C29

C30

C31

C32

C33

C34

C35

C36

C37

C38

C39

C40

C41

C42

C43

C44

C45

Production must be maintained

Production must be maintained

C

C46

C47

C48

C49

C50

C51

C52

C53

C54

C55

C56

C57

C58

C59

C60

C61

C62

Production must be maintained

Have you chosen your job yet?

National Service

National Service

In January 1939 the Government began a national campaign to increase the numbers volunteering in peacetime for service in any future war. The publicity was primarily aimed at securing recruits for the ARP services, but also included information for those who wished to join the reserve forces. All households in the country received copies of a National Service Guide listing the services for which the public could volunteer. The guide and the campaign introduced the term "National Service" to the country and this became the accepted phrase for work of whatever nature in the national interest. Local committees were established to promote all forms of service for the war effort **(D1)**. As part of the drive to raise awareness a **National Service Rally** was held in London's Hyde Park in the early summer of 1939 at which representative volunteers of the ARP, auxiliary and reserve services from throughout the country were on parade. Those attending were issued on the day with a pin back badge indicating on which part of the parade ground they should muster. Some of these badges carry the organisation's initials, others simply a number denoting a corresponding section of the parade ground. Representatives from the Metropolitan Borough of St Pancras for example were issued with badges bearing the number 138. Examples from the **Merchant Navy Reserve (D2)**, and for location number **133 (D3)** are illustrated. An example from the Observer Corps is included with their insignia on page 123.

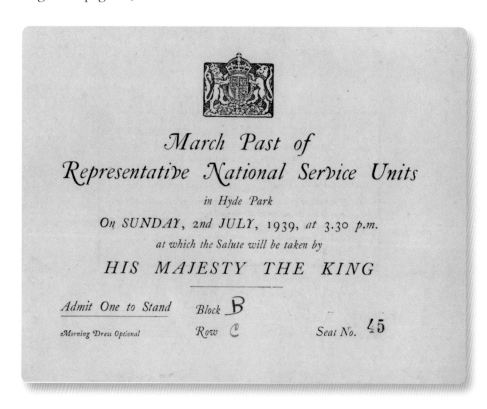

March Past of
Representative National Service Units

in Hyde Park

On SUNDAY, 2nd JULY, 1939, at 3.30 p.m.

at which the Salute will be taken by

HIS MAJESTY THE KING

Admit One to Stand   Block B

Morning Dress Optional   Row C   Seat No. 45

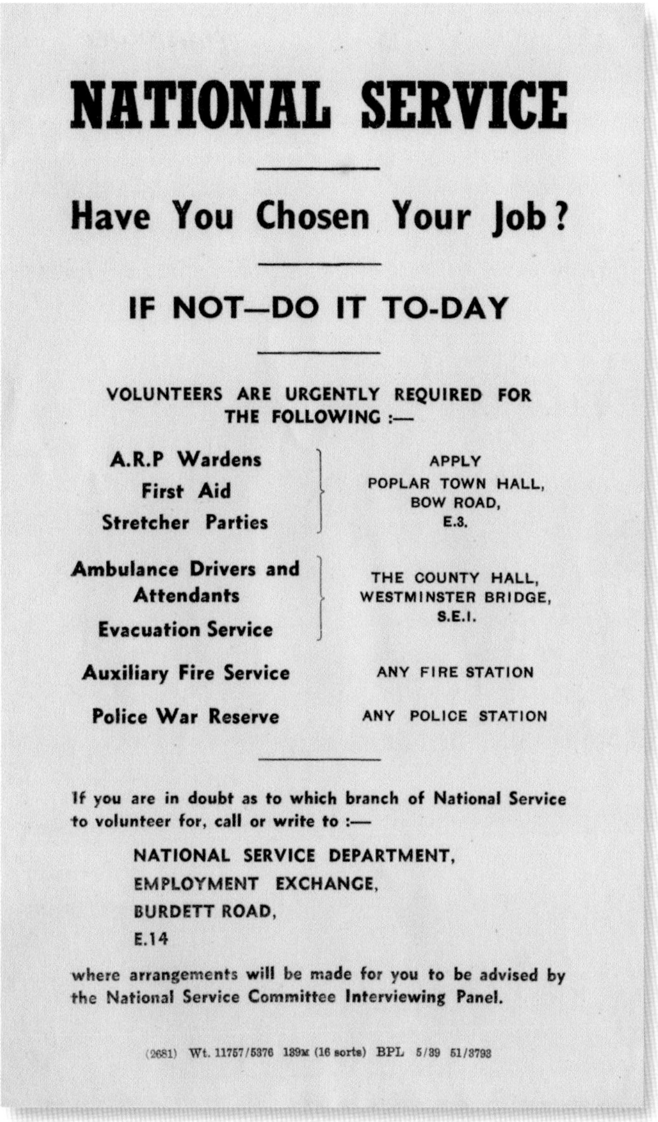

NATIONAL SERVICE

Have You Chosen Your Job?

IF NOT—DO IT TO-DAY

VOLUNTEERS ARE URGENTLY REQUIRED FOR THE FOLLOWING :—

A.R.P Wardens **First Aid** **Stretcher Parties**	APPLY POPLAR TOWN HALL, BOW ROAD, E.3.
Ambulance Drivers and Attendants **Evacuation Service**	THE COUNTY HALL, WESTMINSTER BRIDGE, S.E.I.
Auxiliary Fire Service	ANY FIRE STATION
Police War Reserve	ANY POLICE STATION

If you are in doubt as to which branch of National Service to volunteer for, call or write to :—

NATIONAL SERVICE DEPARTMENT,
EMPLOYMENT EXCHANGE,
BURDETT ROAD,
E.14

where arrangements will be made for you to be advised by the National Service Committee Interviewing Panel.

(2681) Wt. 11757/5376 189m (16 sorts) BPL 5/89 51/8793

Following the example of the reserve forces where, on volunteering, members received a lapel badge, (see page 34), many employers, particularly after the outbreak of war, introduced their own **National Service** badges to denote war service of another kind. These served the same purpose as had the War Service badges of the First World War in ensuring that young men and women in industry were clearly identified as working in the national interest and not available for military service, whilst offering some degree of protection against being offered the white feathers of cowardice handed out to those not in uniform. In the Second War they similarly served to identify those in reserved occupations who were "doing their bit". During the invasion scare in the summer of 1940, these badges were seen as an additional safeguard against infiltration by enemy agents who might disrupt production.

It is not always easy to distinguish between badges from the First War and those from the Second. Whilst the term National Service was preferred, others such as "On War Service" (e.g. the badges from **Halls Barton Ropery (D13)** and the **PTF Mfg Co.** (D14)), "On Essential Work" (e.g. the badge from Chivers **(D18)**), or "Essential War Work" (the badge from **S W Farmer and Co. Ltd (D15)**) were also used in the later period.

In common with the lapels for commercial ARP services, these badges provide a history of British industry and commerce. Many are now difficult to identify with any degree of certainty, although a few contain not only a company name but also a town (e.g. **August's Ltd, Halifax (D16)**, **Southern Aircraft, Gatwick (D17)**), making identification easier.

Some came from companies which in their heyday were, and in many cases still are, household names (e.g. **(D18)** jam makers **Chivers**, **(D19)** shipbuilders and engineers **Thornycroft**, **(D20)** radio makers **Pye** and **(D21)** Guildford-based fire appliance manufacturers **Dennis**). Others are unlikely to be identified without a great deal of research, many simply consisting of a set of company initials **(D22-D27)**. Who for example were **H B B and S** (D24) and which shipping company is represented **(D27)** on the house flag of **S D Co. Ltd**?

Railway Service Badges served the same function for employees of the railway companies and are covered in the section on Transport (see page 218). Workers undertaking the production of stores and munitions directly for the government were usually employed by the Royal Ordnance Factories, whose war service badges are detailed in the next section (see page 66).

D1

D2

D3

D4

D5

D6

D7

D8

D9

Have you chosen your job yet?

Have you chosen your job yet?

D10

D11

D12

D13

D14

D15

D16

D17

D18

D19   D20   D21

D22   D23   D24

D25   D26   D27

Have you chosen your job yet?

The attack begins in the factory

The Royal Ordnance Factories

National Service

Until 1936, when a massive expansion of the production of armaments began in the United Kingdom, three factories were responsible for the government's entire output of munitions for the armed services. These three establishments, jointly known as the **Royal Ordnance Factories (ROFs)** were situated at Woolwich, Enfield and Waltham around the outskirts of London. They had long and distinguished histories - Woolwich could trace its origins to a Royal Laboratory established in 1695. With the threat of an approaching conflict, the government saw that large scale production of war materials would require additional new factories and these were established in areas not vulnerable to air attack, where land was plentiful and where there was likely to be a large pool of labour. For these reasons, many of the factories were established in the depressed areas of the 1930s. ROFs were of three types: explosives factories, engineering factories and filling factories, the last of these having the official title Royal Filling Factories. Between them they manufactured all types of weapons and ammunition, except motor vehicles and tanks which remained the preserve of the motor manufacturing industry. By 1942, the peak of munitions production, there were forty ROFs in production out of a planned total of forty-one. Manpower, from a pre-war total of under 9,000 (the majority at Woolwich) had risen to 300,000 - and seventy per cent of these were women.

As employees wore civilian clothes to and from work and overalls or protective clothing at work, the lapel badge was a common form of identification, primarily as a security measure. The older factories at Woolwich and Enfield had had a system of distinctive badges for some years and these remained in use, the badges for **Woolwich Arsenal (E1)** and the **Royal Small Arms Factory, Enfield (E2)** being illustrated. The former incorporated the arms of the Board of Ordnance, a government body that from the fourteenth century until 1855 had overseen the production of military munitions.

A new system of badges was tested at one of the earliest of the new factories, Nottingham, which began supplementing Woolwich's production of gun parts from 1937. Initial discussions for this badge centred on a design incorporating a coloured background of black, brown, green or mauve depending on the factory type, pinned to the centre of which was a number identifying the individual factory. This proved too complicated and expensive to manufacture and instead a larger variation of the badge worn by workers at Woolwich was produced for all **ROFs** . This again featured the arms of the Board of Ordnance, around which appeared the title "Royal Ordnance Factory" and the factory number. These new badges **(E3)** were introduced from the middle of 1940, but their issue was eventually stopped because of metal shortages, probably around 1942.

Numbers, types and locations have so far only been identified with a degree of certainty for the first sixteen factories, and these are listed below. Some queries still remain with regard to these badges, including exactly how many factories they were issued for. Although one official source states that there were forty-one ROFs, there is definite evidence that an ROF 53 (believed to be at Bridgend in South Wales) existed. There is also a further badge, identical to those above, but with the number replaced by the factory name, e.g. Irvine. These are almost certainly post-war badges, the whole point of the numbering system being to obscure the location of the ROF.

ROF numbered badges and the factories issuing them

ROF Birtley (Cartridge cases)	Badge Number 3
ROF Blackburn (Ammunition fuzes)	Badge Number 4
ROF Cardiff (Engineering)	Badge Number 5
ROF Cardonald	Badge Number 6
ROF Dalmuir (Guns)	Badge Number 7
ROF Fazakerley (Rifles)	Badge Number 8
ROF Leeds (Guns)	Badge Number 9
ROF Hooton (Engineering)	Badge Number 10
ROF Newport (Engineering)	Badge Number 11
ROF Radcliffe (Engineering)	Badge Number 12
ROF Radway Green (Ammunition)	Badge Number 13
ROF Rotherham	Badge Number 14
ROF Wigan	Badge Number 15
ROF Elstow (Filing Factory)	Badge Number 16

* Numbers 1 and 2 have not been positively identified but were possibly Nottingham and Bishopton.

In August 1942 an article in the magazine *War Illustrated* announced that the King had approved a new badge "to be worn by men and women engaged in the Royal Ordnance Filling Factories", to acknowledge the debt owed by the country to those undertaking this dangerous work. The design consisted of two bombs crossed, on the tails of which appeared the letters "ROF" and below a scroll with the inscription "Front Line Duty". The bombs were in silver and the lettering in yellow. This is a very scarce badge, and it may be that it was short-lived, the demand for economy of metals taking hold almost as soon as it was announced. As the issue of the existing ROFs badge was stopped on grounds of metal economy at around this time, it does seem strange to introduce a further metal

The attack begins in the factory

The attack begins in the factory

R·O·F 53 NEWS

No. 15.   MAY, 1943   **Published Monthly.**

FOREWORD

Mrs. R. JONES

Dear Friends,

It is now 2½ years since I started in this factory, and I feel that besides helping my country I have made contact with a jolly set of girls. The unit in which I work resembles one big family. If the same team-work exists in every unit as it does in 3.L.13 our production must go up by leaps and bounds. We feel that we are helping our boys as much as possible to bring the war to a victorious end, which, incidentally, I am positive is the aim of everyone at the factory. Personally, I think this is the best way that I can do my duty towards my country.

Having spent the whole of my 2½ years on the T. & P. Section I and my colleagues find much pleasure and satisfaction in the knowledge that we have helped in building up the vast supply of munitions which are now reaching our boys who are doing their best to clear the oppressed lands.

Looking back over this period I am amazed to find how hard it all seemed to reach the peak of production, but once that peak had been reached how much easier it seems to carry on at that level.

Thanks to the fine co-operation of the inspection we find ourselves still touching the heights in first class production.

Nearly all of us have some dear one who is fighting for us, and so I say "Keep at it R.O.F., and soon our boys will be with us for good, not for leave." My one desire is to continue until the final day when peace shall come once more, when everyone shall live and be happy, and trusting that this is the war to end wars.

Yours faithfully,
R. JONES (Mrs.), 30/416.

— THE MONTH'S THOUGHT —

" Let us have faith that Right makes Might, and in that faith let us to the end dare to do our duty as we understand it."
—Abraham Lincoln.

Flight-Lieut. POOLEY, D.F.C.

Flight-Lieut. POOLEY, D.F.C., Bomber Pilot, visited the factory prior to Easter and gave talks in a number of Canteens. He told of his amazing experiences whilst on operational flights over Germany and Italy, of which he has made over sixty. The most spectacular raid according to this R.A.F. officer was the 1,000 bomber raid on Cologne, in which he and his squadron took part.

He has bombed Berlin, Mannheim, Turin, Brest and many big German and Italian cities.

Flight-Lieut. Pooley said how much the men of the R.A.F. appreciated the work of the factories and pointed out that more, and more, and still more supplies will be needed to support the growing offensive of the Air Force.

His final message before leaving the factory was "I have been around the factory a great deal during the past few weeks and feel sure that all workers must be heartened by the good news from the North African front and I hope this news will serve as some reward for their labours. I wish to thank all workers on behalf of the boys for the fine work you are doing and I hope the war will be over this year."

HOLIDAYS FOR WORKERS

The South Wales and Mon. Council of Social Service has acquired the beautiful premises of "Ivy Towers," Crickhowell, Brecon to serve as a place to which women and children can go for a rest and change.

Crickhowell is a delightful small country town, situated in very beautiful country and is ideal for a quiet change. There are some attractive shops and a cinema.

The sleeping accommodation at "Ivy Towers" is set out in dormitory style and guests will therefore be expected to share rooms. There is a nursery for children and a large and comfortable sitting-room for the use of all guests.

The weekly charges exclusive of travelling expenses are as follows : Adults 25 -; Child (7-14 years) 15 -; Child (under 5) 10 -.

The charges are kept down to a minimum and it is requested that adults make their own and their children's beds and tidy up the dormitories. For all other household work an adequate staff is available.

In addition to changes of clothes and toilet requisites, guests are asked to take for themselves and their children, towels and soap, gas mask, identity cards and ration books.

Applications from women workers who desire to avail themselves of these facilities should be made to the Senior Labour Manager through section officers.

FACTORY "GUY'D" No. 1.
Song Signature.

D.B.V.—"I'll walk beside you."
Proof Yard—"Knock'd 'em in the Old Kent Road."
Smoke—"Smoke gets in your eyes."
Central Stores—"I can't give you anything but love, baby."
Brackla—"Somewhere over the hill."
Labour Dept.—"Questions and Answers."
Pyro—"Where the rainbow ends."
Salvage Dept.—"Any rags, bottles, or bones."
Cordite—"I'll string along with you." Blaze away !
5.H.2—"Where my caravan has rested."
Initiator—"Begin the Beguine."
Burning Ground—"We don't want to set the world on fire."
Laundry—"Oh ! Mr. Wu."
53 Operatic Society—"Be like the kettle and sing."
Road Transport—"I travel the road."
Transport (Rail)—"Wagon Wheels."

badge at this date. A version printed on cloth *(see below)* was worn on the front of overalls, actually a much more sensible distinction in a work environment than a metal badge likely to get caught in machines. Illustrated **(E4)** is a variation of the metal design where the lettering on the tail is "EOF". No reason for this has been uncovered, but two explanations can be advanced. It may have been worn by the staff of the Engineering Ordnance Factories (although the original announcement and the design suggests that it was restricted to filling factories) or it may have been worn at Elstow Ordnance Factory in Bedfordshire, ROF Number 16, which undertook filling duties under the management of J Lyons and Co., the multiple caterers. The factory history refers constantly to the site

as the E.O.F. Two further designs of this badge are also illustrated. In the first **(E5)** the theme of crossed bombs is repeated but superimposed upon them is a red, white and blue roundel of the type painted on RAF aircraft. On this the letters R.O.F. appear across the centre, the letter O outlining the central red section of the roundel. The words "Front Line Duty" appear on an outer scroll around the roundel. In the second variation **(E6)**, the crossed bombs motif more closely resembles crossed artillery shells which are incorporated within an upright rectangular frame with the letters "W.O.F" below. There was a filling factory at Walsall and an explosives factory at Wrexham to which the badge may be appropriate. It is possible that this badge was instituted by the specific ROF after issue of the official badges ceased.

Of interest is the Government issue **On War Service** badge from the First World War **(E8)**, which is usually found in brass bearing the date 1915. The illustrated example was clearly re-issued at the outbreak of war, "1939" being overstamped on the earlier date and a chrome finish applied. Its origins are uncertain, but use by the Royal Ordnance Factories or the naval dockyards is possible.

In common with many commercial concerns, ROFs had their own **Auxiliary Bomb Disposal Squads**, ensuring minimum loss of production through accurate identification of unexploded bombs. Details of the ROF ABDS badge are given on page 108.

Following the massive expansion of the ROFs' capacity in mid-1941 as new factories planned pre-war came on stream, the Engineering ROFs developed a shortage of experienced staff capable of passing on their skills to the new workforce. In July 1941 the Ministry of Supply suggested that the older establishments might lend some of their staff to act as advisers and trainers in the newly created factories. Originally envisaged as a Mobile Skilled Corps, these workers had by September 1941 become known as the ROFs' **National Industrial Mobile Squads (NIMS)**. Working in volunteer teams of fifty these expert fitters, setters, drillers, turners and similar craftsmen were liable for transfer to any provincial ROF for periods of up to one month. The majority of the volunteers came from the ROFs at Woolwich, Enfield and Nottingham. By October 1941, there were 243 volunteers from Woolwich, 127 from Nottingham and 112 from Enfield serving around the country passing on their knowledge. The lapel badge issued to these men **(E7)** consisted of an upright oval in the centre of which appeared the words "Royal Ordnance Factories" in gold lettering on white. Below this in red and blue were the cannons from the arms of the Board of Ordnance. Around the oval appeared a blue circlet with the words "National Industrial Mobile Squad" in gold.

As mentioned earlier, production of military vehicles - tanks and unarmoured vehicles - remained in the hands of the civilian motor manufacturers who before the war made up the British car and lorry industry. These included for example Vauxhall Motors at Luton, responsible for the production of the Churchill tank. Overall production of stores for the armed services had, in July 1939, been placed in the hands of a newly created **Ministry of Supply**. Originally planned as a ministry of munitions to supply the wartime needs of all three services, resistance from the Navy and Air Force resulted in the department concentrating most of its activities on the production of stores for the army and civil defence. Its work with the motor industry required it to oversee the production of fighting vehicles coming from the civilian manufacturers to ensure that the finished product came up to the required standards. For this purpose they established an **Inspectorate of Fighting Vehicles (IFV)** consisting of senior engineering and administrative staff both military and civilian, overseeing the work of the manufacturers in their own factories. In civilian clothes they wore the splendid badge shown **(E9)**, a First World War tank on a chrome ground with the Inspectorate's title around the outside, the colour scheme incorporating the red and yellow chosen as the arm of service colours of the Royal Armoured Corps in 1940.

The motor industry also put its skills to work in the production of military aircraft. By 1939 the government realised that civilian aircraft manufacturers would not by themselves be able to produce all the aircraft required in time of war. To create a division of the ROFs would have been exorbitantly expensive, so again the motor manufacturers were approached. Funded by the government but managed and run by the chosen private firms, **Shadow Factories** were set up by the major manufacturers using the skills of the motor industry to 'shadow' the production of the larger aircraft firms. Illustrated **(E10)** is a badge from the **Austin Motor Company's Shadow Airframe Factory** at Crofton Hackett in the south-west suburbs of Birmingham. The inclusion on this badge of both the factory title and the type of component produced, suggests that it may date from the pre-war re-armament period. Similar breaches of security are illustrated on the badges of the **PMS-T Co. Ltd (E11)**, who under the white ensign of the Royal Navy, proudly announce themselves as 'Admiralty Contractors', and on the national service badge of **Chandlers (E12)** who, with the central device of a bomb, reveal that they manufacture transport and munitions.

E1

E2

E3

E4

E5

E6

E7

E8

E9

E10   E11   E12

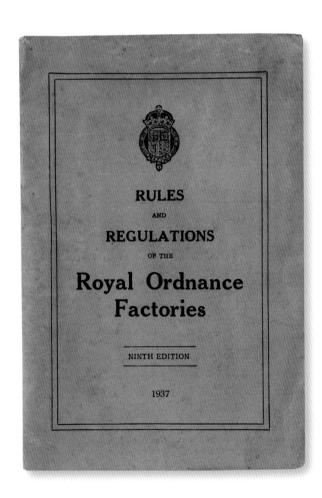

Fall in the fire bomb fighters

The Fire Services

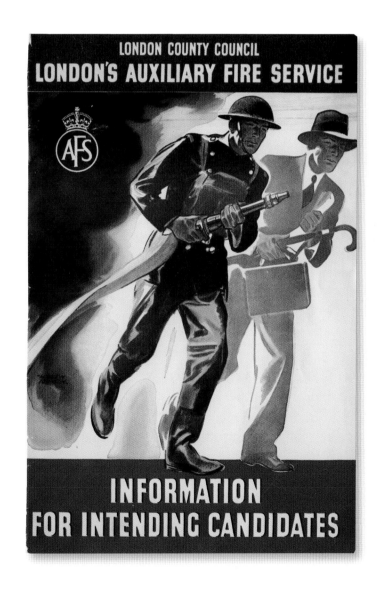

The Fire Services

Perhaps the greatest wartime threat foreseen in the 1930s was the delivery from the air of small incendiary bombs, which dropped in their thousands, would overwhelm the peacetime fire services. The Government's answer was the creation of part-time firemen, trained to augment fire brigades in wartime. These volunteers were known as the **Auxiliary Fire Service (AFS)**, recruitment beginning in 1938.

Like ARP volunteers their services were recognised by the issue of a lapel badge. Details of the badge and the terms for its issue were announced in a Home Office letter of August 1938. Initially they qualified after the completion of sixty hours training, but this was reduced in June 1939 to one month of membership with the aim of boosting recruiting. Designed by a Mr Paget of the Royal Mint the badge **(F1)**, with the letters AFS in red on a circular silver ground surmounted by a crown, was manufactured by J R Gaunt because it contained an enamel surface which the Mint could not produce. The first order was for 45,000 badges, 6,000 of which were to have pin fittings for women volunteers. Initial issues were in sterling silver, but from June 1940 they appeared in white metal. All badges remained the property of the fire brigade authority issuing them and were numbered. Badge Number 1 was presented to the Duke of Kent at a review of the London Fire Brigade and AFS in June 1939. Commercial versions in smaller sizes were also produced **(F2,F3)**, as again, many volunteers felt that the official issue badge was too conspicuous.

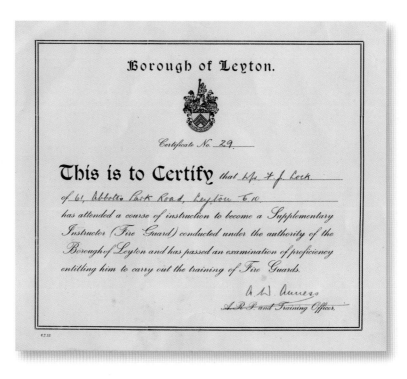

There were surprisingly few variations on this badge. The examples are from the **Ealing Fire Brigade and Auxiliary Fire Service (F6)** and the **Edmonton Auxiliary Fire Service Organisation (F7)**, both designs being based around the traditional fire brigade insignia of helmet and crossed axes, whilst a further pattern is clearly based on the ARP badge but with either a red **(F4)** or blue **(F5)** enamel background.

Following extensive damage caused by fire in the Blitz of 1940-1941, the country's fire services were brought under government control in a **National Fire Service (NFS)**. A new lapel badge **(F8)** was issued for this force based on the AFS badge with the initials changed. The major operational unit of the NFS was the Fire Force, and the **London Fire Force** designed its own badge **(F9)**, which appears in both brass and chrome versions.

Even these augmented fire services could not effectively monitor all buildings for fire danger so civilian volunteers were enlisted to act as a first line of defence. In business premises these **Fire Watchers** were trained to locate and tackle incendiary bombs in the first moments after they fell when they were comparatively easy to extinguish. Although never a government issue, numerous Fire Watcher badges exist and a sample of these **(F10 to F16)** is

illustrated. They range from the elaborate enamel **(F18)** to the simple pin back celluloid **(F16)**. Two of them **(F10, F11)** feature the King's Crown which, unless issued to government organisations was, strictly speaking, illegal.

Commercial companies frequently issued their Fire Watchers with badges of similar design to those of their industrial ARP teams. Illustrated are examples from **MPM (F18)** and **Ransome and Marles (F17)** manufacturers of ball bearings. As with other badges of the period, the quality of these varies enormously. Illustrated **(F26)** is a badge of the simplest sort denoting a **Fire Warden**, yet another example of how the terminology in this area can be very confusing.

The most distinctive badge of this type was, without doubt, that worn by the volunteer fire watchers who protected St Paul's Cathedral in London. The **St Paul's Watch** was a revival of an idea from the First War, consisting of men and women from all walks of life, including many architects, who patrolled the cathedral to protect it from damage. Its badge **(F19)** was designed by sculptor Laurence Turner who had been a member of the watch in the earlier war. Around 280 volunteers served in the St Paul's Watch during the war.

Similar groups of fire-spotting volunteers were recruited in residential districts, initially by Fire Brigades, later as an adjunct to the Warden's Service. When recruited by the Fire Service they were titled **Supplementary Fire Parties**. When working with the Wardens they were known as **Street Fire Parties**. An example of a lapel badge from **Romford** in Essex is shown **(F20)**, together with a simple bar badge **(F21)** on which the letters "S.F.P." appear in blue. Also illustrated **(F22)** is a lapel from an unknown volunteer fire party with the initials "**WAVFP**" which has as its centrepiece the essential tools of the fire party's trade - a bucket, a scoop and a rake. The comparative scarcity of badges for SFPs may be explained by the fact that parties were issued from the outset with an armband as identification or that after the Blitz of 1940-1941 firewatching was a chore that few felt proud enough to boast of doing.

EAST BARNET URBAN DISTRICT.

This is to Certify that

Mr L.D. HOLFORD-STREVENS

23, Somaford Grove

is a member of a **FIRE-FIGHTING PARTY** organised by the East Barnet Urban District Council, and possesses the powers of entry and of taking steps for extinguishing fire or for protecting property, or rescuing persons or property from fire, which are conferred by the Fire Precautions (Access to Premises) (No. 2) Order, 1941.

A.R.P. Controller.

Date of Issue   26 FEB 1942

Number   2210

Signature of Holder

By August 1941 the government had become aware that the various groups of Fire Watchers and SFPs lacked co-ordination and they were replaced by a service of Fire Guards under the control of local authorities. Few badges have been recorded for Fire Guards. This is possibly due to the fact that armbands and later uniforms were issued to members. Illustrated is an example **(F23)** of what may have been a general issue badge, similar in its star-shaped design to the cap badge of the AFS.

In July 1944 badges were authorised for Instructors in the Fire Guard service. Two classes of instructors existed, those trained on national courses, **Instructors, Fire Guard Instructors Course (FGIC)** having a gold coloured background to their badge **(F23)** and those trained locally, Instructors, **Local Fire Guard Instructors (LFGI)** having the design **(F24)** on a silver colour. These badges were authorised, but not an issue, although some local authorities did buy stocks and distribute them free to staff.

F1

F2

F3

F4

F5

F6

F7

F8

F9

Fall in the fire bomb fighters

F10

F11

F12

F13

F14

F15

F16

F17

F18

F19

F20

F21

F22

F23

F24

F25

F26

Fall in the fire bomb fighters

In the Office of Constable

The Police

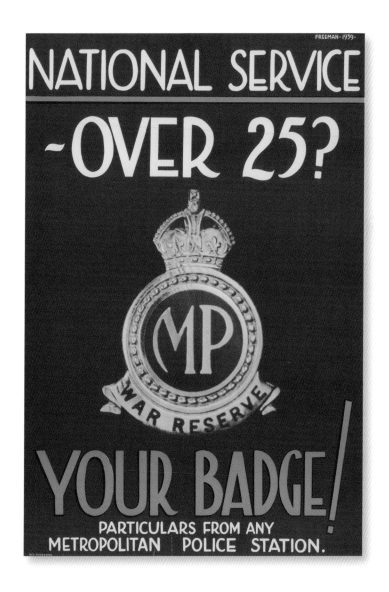

The Police

Prior to the outbreak of the war, there were in the United Kingdom, fifty-eight county police forces and 1231 borough and city-based forces. Many of these were very small - the whole of the county of Oxfordshire for example was policed by just 156 men. Therefore, like the Fire Services, the Police were to be augmented in time of war. Reserve forces would assist in the enforcement of innumerable wartime restrictions and help the newly created Civil Defence services, which in many areas reported directly to the Police.

Two auxiliary forces with established histories already existed. **The Special Constabulary**, a force of unpaid part-time civilian volunteers - dated from the nineteenth century, numbering on the eve of war some 130,000 men. Dating from 1911, the **First Police Reserve** comprised retired police officers who had volunteered to serve again in an emergency in either peace or war. Neither of these forces was ever very large - by 1945 there were only 732 full-time Specials and 2,061 First Reserves in the whole of the UK. Three police organisations however were unique to the wartime period and were eventually to outnumber the original reserves.

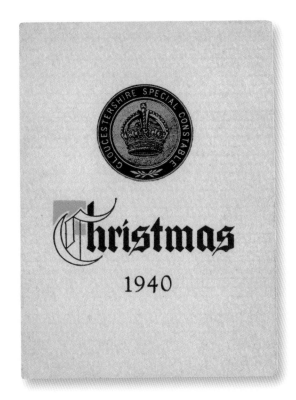

Fearing that the burden of wartime duties would be too great for the existing two reserves, formation of a **Police War Reserve** was announced in 1938. This was to consist of men over thirty recruited for wartime service only, but carrying out the full range of police duties. Initially confined to the Metropolitan and City of London Police forces only it was in March 1939 extended to the whole country. By the end of the war there were over 14,000 War Reserve policemen.

Following representations from womens' organisations, in August 1939 a **Women's Auxiliary Police Corps (WAPC)** was founded, recruiting in the age group eighteen to fifty-five. In the early years of the war their duties ranged from clerical tasks to driving and maintaining motor vehicles, but in many areas they subsequently acquired full police powers. Again, their numbers were never great, just under 4,000 being in service in 1945, but it is interesting to note that by that date, the number of WAPC members with full police powers was three times greater than the number of regular police-women. The Corps was disbanded in 1946, members being given the opportunity to join the regular police if they wished.

Lastly there was the **Police Auxiliary Messenger Service (PAMS)**. This consisted of some five hundred full-time and an unknown number of part-time youths between 16 and 18 years old employed as messengers or in similar jobs with police forces. The service was created in 1940 primarily to allow the young men already

METROPOLITAN POLICE

WOMEN'S AUXILIARY POLICE CORPS

Vacancies exist in the above named Corps at _____ Police Station for women between the ages of 21 and 50 years as telephonists and for general clerical duties.

For further particulars please enquire at this or any Police Station.

M.P. 23869/250 May./1942

serving in these roles to be included in war injuries compensation schemes, which was not possible if they were not members of a formal body. The organisation was put into uniform in 1941 and disbanded in 1945.

In March 1939 the Home Office announced that the King had approved a buttonhole badge for off-duty wear by members of the Special Constabulary who had completed a course of training. This was to consist of a crown surmounting a circular medallion of blue enamel with a silver border. The central device of this could be either the letters SC or a monogram, or letters with a local crest or similar emblem. Numerous examples exist, of which only a small selection **(G1 to G6)** is illustrated.

In October of the same year, use of the buttonhole badge was extended to Police War Reservists and the First Police Reserve, the design being similar to that worn by the Specials with the appropriate lettering. Examples for the **Metropolitan Police War Reserve (G8)** and **Essex Police War Reserve (G9)** are illustrated, suggesting that these Reserves simply added a scroll with the words "War Reserve" to the existing Specials' badge **(see G1 and G2)**.

This scroll commemorates

Constable A. M. Perkins
Bath Special Constabulary

held in honour as one who
served King and Country in
the world war of 1939-1945
and gave his life to save
mankind from tyranny. May
his sacrifice help to bring
the peace and freedom for
which he died.

The example from the **Staffordshire First Police Reserve (G7)** shows the design of the Special's badge again with the lettering changed. The same basic design was subsequently extended to the WAPC **(G10 to G12)** and PAMS **(G13 to G15)** on 5th December 1940. Again, little thought seems to have been given to some of these designs; the **Staffordshire WAPC** badge **(G11)** is identical to that of its Police Reserve with WAPC replacing PR, whilst PAMS badges vary from the letters of the reserve to the inclusion of the city shield on the badge of the **York Police Auxiliary Messenger Service (G15)**.

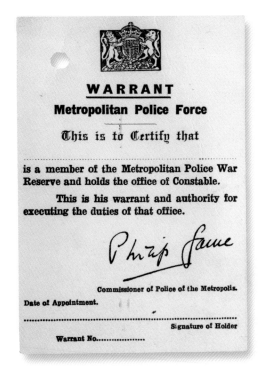

Police Forces were also employed to protect their extensive properties by public services allied to the transport industry where the threat of sabotage as a real danger and transport police forces strengthened to meet wartime threats. Although no record of a separate authority can be traced the **Port of London Authority Police**, responsible for the policing of the London Docks, also issued a badge **(G16)** to their War Reserve, created during 1938 and 1939. This incorporates the PLA arms within a blue border.

Badges for off-duty wear were also authorised in June 1940 for the 900 members of the **Royal Marine Police** and **Royal Marine Police Special Reserve** whose duties included guarding naval dockyards and installations. The Reserve had been established in 1938 for wartime duties along the lines of the other police reserves. The white metal badge **(G17)**, designed by Firmin, was the same for both the main force and Reserve, consisting of a miniature of the globe and laurel cap badge worn in police uniform, itself derived from the collar badge of the Royal Marines. Below this is a bar with the letters "RMP".

A further badge **(G18)** illustrates the close connection of the Police and Special Constabulary with Civil Defence measures. Originating from the Isle of Ely, it incorporates the local coat of arms in blue on white, around which is a blue band with white lettering reading "**Isle of Ely.Special Constabulary.Anti-Gas**". Whether this is a service badge or some form of qualification badge is not known. Its basic method of manufacture does not suggest that it would have been worn on police uniform, and it may therefore have been issued to ARP volunteers trained by the police in anti-gas work.

In the Office of Constable

G

In the Office of Constable

G1

G2

G3

G4

G5

G6

G7

G8

G9

G10

G11

G12

G13

G14

G15

G16

G17

G18

Especially suited to Women

The Ambulance Service

The Ambulance Service

Peacetime ambulance services were not augmented for war in the same way as the Police and Fire Brigades. The services maintained by local authorities were strengthened by the recruitment of part-time auxiliaries, but they formed an integral part of the ARP casualty services of the authority. Their duties involved no requirement for proficiency in first aid as this was provided by the ARP First Aid Parties (in London, Stretcher Parties) who were sent ahead to air raid incidents. Nor were they involved in the normal ambulance work of transporting the sick or attending accidents not due to enemy action. The role of the ARP ambulance service was simply to collect treated casualties from the scene of an air raid and convey them to hospital.

By the outbreak of war there were nearly 12,000 full and part-time local authority ARP ambulances available for service and approximately 16,000 cars (known as sitting case cars) for the conveyance to hospital of the less severely injured. The government had expected the majority of drivers and attendants for the service to be women, but in the event insufficient volunteers came forward and men were also recruited. As a result of the close integration with Air Raid Precautions, ambulance services did not develop a separate identity as did the Police and Fire auxiliary organisations. The majority of the services were entitled to wear the ARP badge (see B1) both in the lapel and later on the cap, so few local authorities went to the expense of producing a separate badge.

The largest of the ARP ambulance services was maintained in London where it came under the control of the London County Council (LCC). Recruitment for what was at first known as the **London Volunteer Ambulance Service (LVAS)** began in October 1938 with a target of 5,000 volunteers. In April 1939 approval was given by the WVS for women trained for the LVAS to wear the WVS badge (see page 114).

A month later a design for a special LVAS badge was submitted by the LCC Supplies Department to the full council for approval. This was to be octagonal, just under 1" x 1" with a transparent amber enamel border and a black enamel centre with the letters "LVAS". These were expected to cost 8½d (4p) each. Unfortunately the Home Office refused to sanction the expenditure insisting that, as noted above, ambulance drivers were eligible for the ARP badge and no separate badge was therefore required.

On the outbreak of war the LVAS was renamed the **London Auxiliary Ambulance Service (LAAS)**. No further action was taken to create an official LAAS lapel badge but in February 1941 the weekly administrative orders for the service noted that "badges and

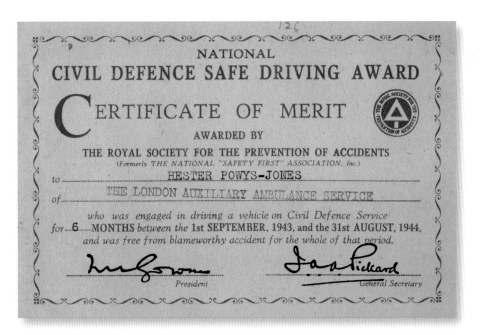

NATIONAL
CIVIL DEFENCE SAFE DRIVING AWARD
CERTIFICATE OF MERIT
AWARDED BY
THE ROYAL SOCIETY FOR THE PREVENTION OF ACCIDENTS
(Formerly THE NATIONAL "SAFETY FIRST" ASSOCIATION, Inc.)
to .... HESTER POWYS-JONES ....
of .... THE LONDON AUXILIARY AMBULANCE SERVICE ....
who was engaged in driving a vehicle on Civil Defence Service
for 6 MONTHS between the 1st SEPTEMBER, 1943, and the 31st AUGUST, 1944,
and was free from blameworthy accident for the whole of that period.

President   General Secretary

brooches bearing a device of a crown and the words `London Auxiliary Ambulance Service' are being worn by members". These **(H1)** consisted of a circular badge surmounted by a crown, divided into three horizontal bars of white, blue and white. The central blue bar featured the words "Auxiliary Ambulance" with the remainder of the service name appearing above and below in the white bars. LAAS orders went on to state that whilst no objection was being raised to the badge, it was not official and was not to be worn on duty or in uniform. A further badge **(H2)** of shield shape and lacking the word "London" is illustrated. It is believed that this may be an earlier version of the one mentioned in 1941.

At least one other local authority thought it worthwhile to issue a special badge for their ARP ambulances. In Leeds, the **Leeds Voluntary Ambulance Corps** sported the lapel badge illustrated **(H3)**, a small oval in green enamel with white metal lettering. Unfortunately nothing is known of this Corps.

An Ambulance Service separate and distinct from the other medical first aid services organised by the local authorities was not always feasible, and in many smaller local authorities all these services were combined into a single Casualty Service, encompassing First Aid Parties, First Aid Posts, Casualty Clearing Stations and the Ambulance Service. Many of the volunteers for these services would have been without any form of uniform until 1941 so the creation of badges such as that **(H4)** for the **County Borough of Smethwick ARP Casualty Service** (incorporating a version of the Red Cross), would not have been unusual.

AN APPEAL
TO WOMEN
Will You
drive to the
Rescue?
LONDON VOLUNTEER
Ambulance Service

H1

H2

H3

H4

Especially suited to Women

...and not a single patient

The Medical and Hospital Services

The Medical and Hospital Services

In common with all the emergency services, hospitals expected that modern war, with widespread and heavy aerial bombardment, would put severe strains on existing resources. To cope with this the country's hospitals, a mixture of private and local authority run, would need to work more closely together than ever before, sharing beds and other valuable resources to care for the expected casualties. To give some idea of the scale of the problem it was estimated that for every ton of high explosive bombs dropped there would be seventy casualties, twenty-four of them deaths. On the eve of war medical services throughout the United Kingdom expected to be faced with a daily tally of 35,000 wounded people claiming their attention.

To cope with this enormous number of casualties the hospital system was in effect nationalised, and the **Emergency Medical Service (EMS)** created. This consisted of the normal hospital staffs carrying out their peacetime tasks, but in greater co-operation with adjoining hospitals in an **Emergency Hospital Scheme**. Overall administration of the scheme was undertaken by officials from the Ministry of Health. The aim, in a city like London, was that air raid casualties occurring in inner boroughs such as Westminster, would receive immediate treatment in the nearest hospital, but be transferred quickly to associated outer London hospitals away from danger. This would then free the inner London beds for the further casualties expected from subsequent raids. Some hospitals chose to mark the existence of the Emergency Hospital Scheme with special badges, although it is not certain exactly what were the qualifications for their issue. Two examples are illustrated, the first **(J1)** having no clue as to its origins, the second **(J2)** being for London's **Hammersmith Hospital**.

The expected casualties also called for an augmentation of nursing staff. In April 1939 the government announced the formation of a **Civil Nursing Reserve** whose members would work as staff in hospitals and first aid posts and help district nurses with evacuation. The scope of the service was later extended to include nursing at medical aid posts in air raid shelters and rest centres. Three levels of staff were recruited :- trained nurses; assistant nurses - those only partially trained, but who already earned their living by nursing - and nursing auxiliaries (civilian volunteers who received a fortnight's training). In February 1943, the reserve supplied to hospitals 3,200 trained nurses, 2,800 assistant nurses and 12,800 auxiliaries. It was announced in December 1945 that the Reserve would remain in existence for some time after the war to meet a shortage of nursing staff.

In June 1940 authority was issued for a CNR membership badge to be worn on the left side of the indoor uniform. The badge **(J3)** was issued free when members registered for service. In November an outdoor uniform was authorised and the badge was taken into use as a cap badge. The design comprised a shield on which appeared the words "Civil/Nursing/Reserve" surmounted by a crown. A similar badge without the crown, with the title in full and the letters "NA" in red script below is also recorded, but its exact use is unknown.

As ARP ambulances were mainly crewed by women there was a need for men to unload stretchers from the vehicles, move the casualties around hospitals and load them onto transport for removal to safer areas. Hospitals therefore anticipated the need for a greatly increased number of stretcher bearers. In April 1940 they were given authority to recruit **Voluntary Stretcher Bearers** who were issued with a basic uniform of overalls. Later that year a lapel badge **(J4)** was authorised. This took the form of the letters SB surmounted by a crown with, below the letters, two scrolls and the words "Emergency Hospital Scheme". Some supplies of the badge were obtained through the Post Office Stores Department. By the end of the war there were 25,000 stretcher bearers in England and Wales and 4,000 in Scotland.

Domestic work in hospitals - cooking and cleaning - is not glamorous at the best of times. Voluntary domestic work in wartime is even less so, but there was a great need for such help and hospitals encouraged women unable to take a more active role to volunteer for this as their war work. To acknowledge this contribution and hopefully to act as a stimulus to the recruitment of further volunteers, a badge **(J5)** was approved in October 1941 for all volunteer domestic staff giving part-time **Hospital Service** for over 96 hours per month. In April 1942 issue of the badge was extended to all hospital staff except doctors or nurses. Between December 1941 (when compulsory registration of women for war work began) and May 1943, nearly 24,000 people were directed to hospital domestic work.

The badge issued was circular, with the words "Ministry of Health" in silver on red around the edge, a central bar bearing the words "Hospital Service". A press item which appeared at the time of issue stated that the wording on the bar was to be "Hospital Staff", but is not known if this was a mistake or whether it records an early version. There exists a further version of this badge where the red enamel is replaced by blue and the circle is surmounted by a King's crown, but the reason for this variation is not known.

Two similar badges subsequently appeared for Ministry of Health and local authority staff in **Evacuation Nurseries (J6)** and **Evacuation Hostels (J7)**. The former had originated as an offshoot of the evacuation scheme in 1939, but their importance had grown as more and more women replaced men in industry, leaving them little time to care for small children. These nurseries, looking after children from two to five years old, eventually provided over 16,000 places in nearly 400 nurseries, many open fifteen hours a day. The hostels had similarly been conceived as a means of removing from danger pregnant women prior to their admission to maternity hospitals. Again their role expanded as the war continued, with some one hundred and twenty five hostels with 2,100 beds existing in late 1944. In the two badges authorised for these services, the title again appeared on the central bar whilst the outer circle had a blue background rather than the red ground of the hospital badge.

Pre-war planning of the medical services had envisaged that the large number of expected casualties would quickly overwhelm even the augmented hospitals if some further form of assistance was not provided. Within the ARP services therefore a service of local **First Aid Posts (FAPs)** was created, designed to treat the lightly wounded who

AIR RAID PRECAUTIONS.   Cert. No. 215.

Local Certificate of First Aid Training.

This is to Certify *that*   T/³ Culling,

Burghclere School House, Nr Newbury,

has completed a **COURSE OF FIRST AID TRAINING** *held under the auspices of*

the Kingsclere & Whitchurch Rural District Council,

and has acquired a sufficient knowledge of First Aid to act as a member of a public Air Raid Precautions Service.

Nature of Course attended   First Aid Full Course.

Name and Qualification of Instructor   Dr F Kendall.

Dated   12° June, 1939   **Signed**

On behalf of Local Authority.

Chairman of the A.R.P. Committee.

Ex^d.

(This Certificate is to be regarded as of Local validity only).

did not require hospital attention. These FAPs were administered by the Ministry of Health and staffed by volunteers, many from the uniformed sections of the Red Cross or St John Ambulance Brigade, or by members of the CNR. If not already in uniform as members of these bodies, an ARP uniform was provided, the trained member being eligible for the ARP badge (see B1).

At least one FAP seems to have supplemented this with its own distinctive insignia shown in the badge **(J8)** from the **Pool Street FAP** with its Latin motto, "Semper Paratus" (Always Ready). Neither the area nor origin of this badge is know, although as FAP staff were not eligible for an ARP outdoor uniform, it seem possible that it was issued for wear on the civilian clothes of the Pool Street volunteers when off duty.

Treatment for the physical wounds of an air raid casualty received much thought in pre-war planning, but for one section of the community their spiritual welfare required as much attention. In October 1938 the magazine *First Aid*, announced that a badge had been designed to be worn by Roman Catholics in wartime. Made in celluloid onto a tin backing, the badge **(J9)** was circular with the words '**In case of injury call a Catholic Priest**' around the edge. The central device was a cross, on either side of which were the letters 'RC'. To cover all eventualities, there was a version of this badge printed on rubber with an adhesive backing, which was designed to be stuck to the rubber facepiece of a gas mask.

L.E.C. No. 35 (B)   Reg. No. C.5531.

CITY OF MANCHESTER

*Local Emergency Committee
for the
Nursing Profession*

CIVIL NURSING RESERVE

Membership Card

Category

NURSING AUXILIARY

J1

J2

J3

J4

J5

J6

J7

J8

J9

...and not a single patient

If you are bombed out

The Post-Raid Services

AFTER THE RAID!
CITY OF MANCHESTER

It might be YOU!

The Post-Raid Services

Well in advance of the war, the government had anticipated the damage and casualties which might be caused in air raids by explosives and fire and created services to alleviate them. What had not been expected was the widespread disruption of normal life as large numbers of families were displaced following the destruction of their homes. Those preparations which had been made proved inadequate for the numbers of people needing help. As a result there came into existence, or developed on existing services a range of agencies to assist those whose homes had been destroyed or damaged and who needed help and advice to regain some measure of normal life.

The first port of call for those "bombed out" was the **Rest Centre**. Local authority staff, many drafted in from other jobs and working in requisitioned buildings such as schools, provided shelter for the homeless until they felt able to move on and pick up the threads of everyday life. In these centres they found a place to sleep, basic food and, as the services developed, help and advice. No uniforms were authorised for local staff, although armlets and lapel badges were, the example illustrated **(K1)** being the most commonly encountered, although nothing is known of its origins. Many local authorities issued their own designs of these and examples of lapels from several are illustrated **(K2 to K6)**, some including the title "Air Raid Welfare", which suggests they were probably issued more widely than just to rest centre staff. Paid staff were frequently assisted by voluntary helpers, many from the WVS and two examples of similar badges from Tyneside **(K7,K8)** are shown. In Scotland, from December 1940, these services were known as the **Emergency Relief Organisation**, whose duties encompassed a wide range of post-raid tasks including Rest Centres and lapel badges were issued.

The London County Council (LCC) sought authority to issue a badge to those working in its centres in August 1940. This was to consist of a small celluloid buttonhole badge bearing the letters "R.C.V" for Rest Centre Volunteer with the LCC coat of arms above. Authority was given for the purchase of 2,500 of these at under one penny each on the 28th of the month, but there is no indication as to whether the order was ever placed.

From July 1942, by which time the service had matured enormously from the chaotic days of the Blitz, the Ministry of Health issued a national badge to all workers in Rest Centres. This followed the design of the badge issued to hospital and nursery staff (see J5), in consisting of a white enamel circle on which appeared the words "Rest Centre Service" in silver lettering. Across the centre of the badge was a horizontal bar with the name of the issuing local authority in blue. The only recorded example for England bears the county name "Gloucestershire". A similar badge issued to the separate service in Scotland has "Scotland" on the bar.

After recovering from their initial shock, the homeless needed to visit a number of local and central government agencies to collect the essentials of life, from ration books and new clothes to identity cards and money. At first these agencies operated from their peacetime offices with the result that the homeless often had to travel great distances to pick up the pieces of their shattered lives. By late 1940 however many local authorities had established one central location where representatives of all the services were gathered together.

For overall advice on their rights, the bombed out could turn to a representative of the **Citizens Advice Bureaux**. Before the war the National Council of Social Service and voluntary groups associated with it had planned to establish an advice and information service for the citizen and the first bureau came into operation on 4th September 1939. The Bureaux' workers offered discussion of and advice on the problems of those attending the centres, made them aware of their entitlements and how to contact and make the best of the services available. By 1942 there were over 1,000 bureaux, 90 per cent of the staff for which were volunteers. Workers on this war service were issued with the badge shown **(K9)**, a blue oval with the lettering in gilt.

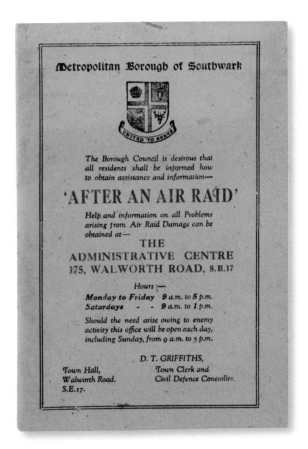

Metropolitan Borough of Southwark

UNITED TO SERVE

The Borough Council is desirous that all residents shall be informed how to obtain assistance and information—

'AFTER AN AIR RAID'

Help and information on all Problems arising from Air Raid Damage can be obtained at—

THE ADMINISTRATIVE CENTRE 175, WALWORTH ROAD, S.E.17

Hours :—
Monday to Friday   9 a.m. to 5 p.m.
Saturdays   -   -   9 a.m. to 1 p.m.

Should the need arise owing to enemy activity this office will be open each day, including Sunday, from 9 a.m. to 5 p.m.

D. T. GRIFFITHS,
Town Hall,   Town Clerk and
Walworth Road.   Civil Defence Controller.
S.E.17.

If the bombed out family had members in the services they might seek advice or assistance from the representative of the **Soldiers, Sailors and Airmens Families Association**, almost always abbreviated to **SSAFA**. These workers would take family details, ensure that the servicemen were informed of the family's situation and advise on benefits available. Two lapels are illustrated **(K10, K11)**.

Outside the Rest Centres responsibility for informing the population of the emergency measures taken for their protection was delegated to **Ministry of Information Emergency Committees**. The Ministry itself had been formed at the outbreak of war to ensure that official information was passed accurately and speedily to all who needed it. At local level it worked through voluntary committees made up of representatives of organisations such as trades unions, churches and local newspapers. After a raid or under conditions of invasion, these committees were to advise the public, by means of posters and loudspeaker vans, of the location of rest and advice centres, the safety of water and gas supplies and the availability of emergency food.

They were not uniformly successful at their job and in many cases were considered by local authorities to be ineffective, but in some areas they did their utmost to overcome the disastrous circumstances which many of the raids created. No uniforms were necessary and committee members were identified by the lapel badge shown **(K12)**.

A further eventuality not foreseen was the large number of high explosive bombs dropped which failed to explode, causing widespread disruption to civilian life and the loss of many hours of valuable industrial production. The Army, responsible for all unexploded bombs (UXBs) on land, initially had few men to spare for the task and were overwhelmed by the numbers to be dealt with. As a consequence the time taken to remove UXBs could be considerable.

One government department which found these delays unacceptable was the Ministry of Aircraft Production (MAP), struggling to replace valuable aircraft destroyed by enemy action. In the summer of 1940 the Ministry had set up a Factory Defence Section to co-ordinate plans for the protection of their premises against sabotage or invasion. In December 1940 they extended this role by suggesting to manufacturers on their list that they establish **Auxiliary Bomb Disposal Units** (usually known as ABD squads or **ABDS**) to be recruited from factory personnel. The function of an ABDS was to search factory premises after raids, detect any UXBs, clear and mark danger zones around bombs found, report these to the proper authorities, do any necessary preparatory work (possibly including digging down to the bomb) and then assist the Royal Engineer Bomb Disposal unit once they arrived in any way required. The aim of this work was to prevent false reports of bombs in factories and thus minimise the disruption to production.

Although initially the scheme applied only to factories with 500 or more employees, the principle was gradually extended to a variety of production departments and to some public utility undertakings. By 1943 there were fifty-nine companies with ABDS in the

London Civil Defence Region and some 132 throughout the country, the majority of their members trained at the Bomb Disposal School at RAF Melksham in Wiltshire. Squad strengths varied from six men to around thirty. The original MAP note suggested that "Members generally should be of the mechanic or labourer type rather than clerical or executive". From September 1942 all Auxiliary Bomb Disposal Units were incorporated into their local Home Guard battalions. Serving members were given two weeks to decide if they wished to enlist in the Home Guard. After this date, ABDS wore Home Guard uniform with a distinctive cloth badge on the lower left arm of their battledress. Two lapels for ABDS are shown, one from the **Royal Ordnance Factories (K13)**, the other from **Vickers-Armstrong (K14)**. There must be many more of these, although the numbers employed in this work by each factory suggests that they are unlikely to be common.

LONDON'S AWAKE!

SEPTEMBER 16th, 1940   NUMBER 7

PUBLISHED WEEKLY BY THE LONDON REGIONAL OFFICE
MINISTRY OF INFORMATION

NOTE: The aim of London's Awake is to give to the members of Local Information Committees, Information Officers and the other workers in the London Region, speaking points and ideas which they may pass on, and to be a link between them and our Office.

COUNTY HALL, S.E.1.

HERE is the "blitzkrieg," except that for us there has been no "blitz" about it. We were prepared for it physically, mentally and morally. And far from having a disintegrating effect on the people of London, it has closed their ranks still further. Civil defence personnel, the members of all the "auxiliary" forces, W.V.S. Housewives Service, shelter marshals, official and improvised, etc. etc. together with the general public—all are presenting an unbroken front to the fire and fury in the skies. And what about Local Information Committees and Information Officers? During the last two days we have directed their attention to the following points :—

(1) Listen carefully to broadcasts about air raids in the London Area and note the main points for conveyance to others;

(2) Know the address of the temporary accommodation for evacuated persons in your area, and generally be familiar with any emergency measures adopted in case the authorities ask for your help;

(3) Vigorously talk down rumour or exaggeration which you have been able to check by your own observation;

(4) Report to the Secretary of the Local Information Committee at once any matters about which the public are particularly anxious;

(5) Above all, go around your area as much as possible, and use your personal influence.

We have suggested that the Information Officers might occasionally talk to the audience now nightly to be found in large numbers in shelters. I find as I go about in my own borough that a talk about the situation, and such explanations as one can offer about obscure points, are very welcome. Rumour is rife in the conditions in which we now find ourselves ; and rumour must be extinguished with as much rapidity and skill as the incendiary bomb. For, to pursue the metaphor further, it does not burn itself out but spreads. The extinguisher is the Information Officer ; and the means he employs are facts when he can get them, and when he can't, the rather daunting question "Who told you so?" or "What's your evidence?" We shall do our best to provide Local Committees with facts and explanations about certain questions, e.g., the (to most people) mysterious evolutions of enemy aircraft at night, and we shall rely on Information Committees to let us know about what matters further information and explanation is needed. There is much that Information Officers can do by using their own common sense. For example, an enterprising Information Committee would get hold of the local Press reporter and feature any street shelter which has stood up well to a high-explosive bomb; and there are plenty. And yet these "surface" shelters are in many places little used. There are many other ways in which steps can be taken, things said, and words spoken which have a clarifying and steadying effect; and to be out to do that of set purpose is just what Information Officers have been enrolled to do.

Wyndham Deedes

K1

K2

K3

K4

K5

K6

K7

K8

K9

K10

K11

K12

K13

K14

The Ladies in green

The Women's Voluntary Services

The Women's Voluntary Services

Established in 1938 the **Women's Voluntary Services for Air Raid Precautions (WVS)** were an attempt to encourage women to join the newly created ARP services and prepare themselves for service in war. Gradually, under the leadership of their charismatic chairman Lady Reading, they undertook a much wider range of tasks related to the war effort. Starting with assistance during the evacuation of 1939 they eventually involved themselves in most aspects of the Home Front. A full list of their activities in 1943 is given in the Appendix on page 265. By February 1939, they had recognised this gradual change of role and amended their title to the **Women's Voluntary Services for Civil Defence**.

It was not originally envisaged that the WVS would wear any form of uniform and a lapel badge was introduced to be worn with civilian clothes. The design, by Marples and Beasley of Birmingham, consisted of the title of the organisation in red letters on a white metal upright rectangle, the whole surmounted by a King's crown.

Metropolitan Borough of Lambeth

— WOMEN'S VOLUNTARY — SERVICE FOR CIVIL DEFENCE

For the purpose of advising women and stimulating their interest in the work of the various Civil Defence Services, for which the Council are responsible, and which are described in the "Guide to National Service," a local branch of the above voluntary organisation has been established at :—

74 ALEXANDRA DRIVE
(near Gipsy Hill Station)
UPPER NORWOOD, S.E. 19

Office Hours :
MONDAYS, WEDNESDAYS and FRIDAYS
3 p.m. to 5 p.m. and 6 p.m. to 8 p.m.
TUESDAYS and THURSDAYS
11 a.m. to 1 p.m.

Information and assistance can be obtained from Mrs. A. A. CAPPER, the Local Executive Officer, at the above address

Telephone No.: GIPsy Hill 3467

O. L. ROBERTS
Town Clerk and Chief Executive Officer
Lambeth Air Raid Precautions Scheme
LAMBETH TOWN HALL
BRIXTON HILL, S.W. 2

It was issued only to those who had volunteered for service and then undertaken a series of lectures "to prepare themselves to carry out their duties". The first pattern badge **(L1)** gave prominence to the letters ARP over the organisation title, but that issued from February 1939 **(L2)** had the letters WVS with the words "Civil Defence" below. A third pattern of this badge with the letters WVS without a sub-title is a post-war pattern worn from 1947 to about 1950, when Civil Defence duties were temporarily dropped from the WVS role.

In June 1939 a standard greatcoat became available for members who wished to purchase it, and instructions were issued that the badge was to be worn on the left lapel of this. In April 1940, when bar brooches for rank were introduced (see below), instructions were revised so that in future the badge was to be worn only in the newly introduced felt hat. From February 1941 a green beret was available as an alternative to the felt hat and the metal badge was authorised for wear in this as well, although a cloth badge was suggested as a more suitable alternative.

Originally the WVS prided itself that it did not have a rank structure, but this principle was amended in April 1940 by the issue of bar brooches **(L3)** on which appeared the "rank" or appointment of the wearer. These, all of a similar style, consist of a white metal bar into which the title of the wearer is embossed in red lettering. The lettering colour varies from the deeper maroon of the WVS colours through to a much brighter red. In uniform these brooches were worn on the right lapel of the overcoat or jacket. Members without uniform wore the brooch immediately below the WVS badge on the left lapel.

Brooches were originally authorised for - **Regional Administrator, Regional Organiser, County Organiser, Centre Organiser** and **Headquarters Staff** but others were subsequently added. In March 1941 came brooches for **Area Organiser** and **Regional Staff**. By April 1942 brooches also existed for **County Staff** and **County Borough Organiser**, the latter being required to pay 3/- (15p) for their new badges and having to hand in their Centre Organiser badges to get it.

By the end of 1941 a consolidated list of badges includes all the above as well as **Assistant County Organiser** and two badges unique to Scotland, **Large Burgh Organiser** and **Large Burgh Staff**, a Burgh being the Scottish equivalent of an English Borough. Other brooches exist for which no authority has been traced, including one marked **Dep Centre Organiser**.

One further WVS pin back badge was manufactured. This is a white metal monogram of the letters WVS **(L4)** worn at the neck of the blouse when in uniform. It appears in official records in June 1941 and is listed as available for purchase from WVS headquarters in December 1942, but no date of introduction has been traced.

WVS Housewives Service

It was recognised from the creation of the WVS that many women willing to work for the Service had domestic or family commitments which would prevent them from doing so full time. It was felt that these women could be of particular service to air raid wardens in their districts by having detailed knowledge of the residents of their streets and assisting with the care of casualties at an incident before the arrival of the first aid services.

The title of **Housewives Service** for these on-call volunteers, originated in Barnes on the outskirts of London in early 1940 and quickly spread throughout London Region and later the country. By 1943 there were 265,000 members of the service nation-wide.

The most commonly encountered badge for the service is the octagonal design illustrated **(L5)**. This also exists in a version with light green enamel top and bottom rather than blue, but it is not known if this is simply a manufacturer's variation or whether the change of colour has some significance. A version issued to service members in Bristol **(L6)** is circular and made of a pressed card which resembles leather, the designation being embossed in gold lettering on a maroon ground.

WVS Salvage Work

In July 1940 local authorities were asked to set up schemes for the salvage of raw materials for the war effort, and many areas left detailed implementation to the WVS. In fact, the WVS had already been asked by the government in February to get involved in salvage and lapel badges naturally followed. In some areas, individual badges were issued by the WVS to identify their own collectors, although as schemes became more organised with local authorities issuing their own badges (see page 177) separate WVS ones became less common. Examples from a Bristol manufacturer are shown **(L7, L8)**, although it is not known if their use was confined to that area. These badges are made in card with a leather effect coloured surface. Two colours are depicted but others exist in light brown, red or green. The significance of these colours is not known.

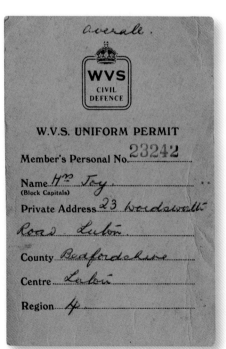

In 1942 the WVS approached local education authorities in London with a view to involving schoolchildren in the collection of salvage as **Junior Salvage Stewards**. In order to make the campaign of more interest to children, badges were issued - the design **(L9)** representing a cog wheel - to be awarded to the keenest workers. The **Cogs Scheme** eventually became nation-wide involving salvage posters designed by the children and a Cogs Song entitled "There'll Always be a Dustbin". Normally the Cogs worked with members of the WVS or other adults, but in some areas they organised salvage collections entirely by themselves.

L1

L2

L3

L4

L5

L6

L7

L8

L9

The Ladies in green

Forewarned is Forearmed

The Royal Observer Corps

The Royal Observer Corps

By 1939 the coastline of Britain was protected against surprise aerial attacks by a chain of radar stations detecting incoming aircraft and alerting the defences. These stations however were only capable of monitoring aircraft out to sea. Once over land the tracking of aircraft became the responsibility of the specialist volunteers of the **Observer Corps**.

This Corps originated with the air defence organisation of the First World War which, disbanded at the end of hostilities, had been revived in 1925 as part of the UK's air defences. Corps members were enrolled as special constables and administered by county police forces. During the late 1930s the importance of the Corps was recognised and expansion took place. Its activities were included in the National Service guide of 1939, with members taking part in the rally in London (see page 58) in that summer. A badge for that occasion is illustrated **(M1)**. Called out for full time service on the outbreak of war, responsibility for the Corps passed from the Police to the Air Ministry, although technically members remained Special Constables.

Granted the title **Royal Observer Corps** in April 1941 in recognition of its service in the preceding years, sweeping changes took place in 1943. These included the introduction of official training, a graded rank structure and the increased employment of women. Uniforms were introduced for all ranks.

In June 1944 specially recruited observers from the Corps were stationed on the ships of the Allied invasion fleet to ensure correct recognition of both enemy and friendly aircraft. By May 1945 when the Corps was stood down, 1,400 observer posts covered the skies over the United Kingdom.

As a civilian organisation the Corps in the 1920s and 1930s had no uniform, although a version of the police duty armband was worn when manning posts. In October 1929 it was announced that a lapel badge was to be issued on repayment to observers awarded certificates of proficiency. The badge **(M2)**, in white metal with a light blue outer band containing the corps title, depicted an Elizabethan coastwatcher scanning the horizon and holding aloft a flaming torch. The designer of the badge is unknown. Two further versions exist, one all in white metal **(M3)**, the other, less common with the outer band in royal blue. The significance of these variations, if any, is not known.

During the period up to 1943, there was no official training syllabus for Observer Corps volunteers, resulting in a variety of training aids and publications to assist the keen

volunteer to identify aircraft. This subject became very popular with schoolboys, resulting in the formation of a **National Association of Spotters Clubs (NASC)**, the majority of the affiliated organisations being spotters clubs in schools or pre-service cadet units. The NASC badge consisted of an aircraft in flight above a city roofscape, with the letters "NASC" below, the whole design in gilt on blue.

In June 1940 with the threat of invasion, observers were issued with a uniform of RAF pattern overalls and a blue woollen beret, the qualification badge appearing on the beret as a cap badge. The change of title in 1941 brought about a revised lapel badge **(M4)**. The new title was incorporated in the blue band and a King's crown surmounted the circle. A smaller version of this badge **(M5)** with a chromed rather than white metal finish is almost certainly a post-war issue.

Revived after the war with a much changed role in the age of nuclear warfare, the Corps was finally disbanded in 1993.

ROYAL OBSERVER CORPS
CERTIFICATE OF WAR SERVICE

This certificate is awarded by the Air Council as an expression of their high appreciation of the war services rendered to the Royal Air Force by   Observer M. L. William *as a member of the Royal Observer Corps*

Stansgate

SECRETARY OF STATE FOR AIR

JANUARY 1946

M1

M2

M3

M4

M5

Forewarned is Forearmed

If the Invader comes

The Home Guard and Invasion Defence

"COR! PARATROOPS!!"

The Home Guard and Invasion Defence

The Home Guard

On 10th May 1940 German forces invaded Holland and Belgium. In their lightning attacks they made extensive use of parachute and airborne troops, often landing far behind the defending forces. British military authorities realised that if similar landings took place in the United Kingdom, there were insufficient troops in the rear areas to guard against this threat. Their answer was to create a force of local volunteers who would report on the arrival of enemy troops and where possible, fight to resist them.

No. ⟨E2A/160/1

Has been enrolled as a Member of " E " Company, Broxton Group Local Defence Volunteers.

Lieut. Colonel
Company Commander

Date 23/6/40

On the evening of 14th May the Secretary of State for War, Anthony Eden broadcast an appeal for men between the ages of seventeen and sixty-five to join a new force to be known as the **Local Defence Volunteers**. By 20th May this numbered over 250,000 men.

On the 23rd July, following an initiative by the Prime Minister, the name was changed to the **Home Guard**.

The force remained in existence until 1st November 1944 when it stood down, a German invasion no longer being a threat. It was finally disbanded in December 1945. By stand down the force was some 1,727,000 strong including women auxiliaries. Its members had served as infantry, coast and anti-aircraft gunners and in a variety of other specialist roles including bomb disposal.

Commercial badge manufacturers were quick to seize on this new opportunity for a lapel badge. Although discussed, no official badge was ever designed or issued, so all are the product of the civilian badge designers. (An official looking badge with the letters HG, similar to that issued to the TA, is a post-war issue to the revived Home Guard of that period). A proposal from the War Office after the war to issue badges to ex-members of the Home Guard was not pursued.

No lapel badges for the Local Defence Volunteers have been recorded and it seems likely that in the seventy days of their existence there was insufficient time for the manufacturers to produce any.

The most frequently encountered design is a simple oval of coloured enamel, usually blue, on which the letters HG appear in gilt, a crown with red cushion surmounting the oval **(N1)**. There is also a version entirely in white metal, possibly a later war economy version. From its use in official publications this is probably the nearest to an approved standard design. Three variations appeared on this badge, two probably on stand down as commemorative badges. All have the standard design, two having added dates of service. One **(N10)** has "1940-1-2-3" the other **(N11)** "1940-4". The third design **(N12)** has attached below it five inverted red enamel chevrons of the type introduced in February 1944 for wear on the sleeve of the battledress blouse, each chevron indicating one completed year of war service.

Examples of other designs based around the initials are illustrated **(N2 to N6)**, including one made in sterling silver **(N5)**. Two designs with red and white backgrounds were also used **(N4, N6)**, the tablets being similar to those used in commercial versions of the ARP and AFS badges (see B4, F5). Less common are designs with the force title in full **(N7 to N9)**, one appearing to incorporate a lion. That with the blue rectangular tablet and the wording Home Guard in full **(N9)** was worn by the author's grandfather as a member of the 28th County of London (Wandsworth) Battalion.

Many counties and units went to the expense of producing designs incorporating the regimental cap badges authorised for wear by Home Guard battalions in August 1940. Illustrated are examples from **Kent (N13)** where the county's white horse badge appears on a background of the regimental colours of the Queen's Own Royal West Kent Regiment, from Scotland, where the **9th (Post Office) Battalion of the Glasgow Home Guard**, incorporated the badge of the Highland Light Infantry and the battalion designation **(N14)** and from **Northamptonshire**, where the title "Home Guard" has been added to the County regimental cap badge **(N15)**.

A similar concept has been followed with the badge from the **Warwickshire Home Guard (N16)**, where the letters "HG" have been added below the county regiment's antelope. The two designs worn by **County of Lancaster Home Guard** battalions **(N17,N18)** give both the battalion number and the design of the cap badge worn in those units: - the grenade of the Lancashire Fusiliers in the case of the 42nd (Salford) Battalion and the fleur-de-lys of the Manchester Regiment in the case of the 49th

(Manchester) Battalion. Lancashire had battalions numbered from 1 to 93 (with gaps in the sequence) and it would be interesting to know if all the battalions had similar badges.

Units of the Home Guard were also raised by commercial concerns to guard vulnerable points such as factories, although most were subsequently incorporated into local general service battalions. Three designs are shown, the largest **(N19)** being for an unidentified Home Guard Works Unit, which incorporates the King's crown. The two units badged to the South Staffordshire Regiment were raised by companies within the county, **Metro-Cammell (N20)** and **The Patent Shaft Company (N21)**.

During 1940 all the major railway companies created Home Guard units to protect their installations and working lines, but none seem to have produced lapel badges for them. There is in existence a lapel badge for the **London Transport Home Guard (N22)**, whose members protected bus garages and railway depots. The design shows the LT griffin superimposed on the Maltese cross cap badge of the King's Royal Rifle Corps, worn by many London Home Guard battalions. Also shown are the infamous pikes issued to the Home Guard at one point in its existence. Inclusion on the design of the dates 1940-1945 indicates however that it must be a post-war old comrades badge. There would appear to be several variations of this badge, with the battalion number varying in each case. LT raised seven London battalions numbered 41,42,43,44,45,46 and 60.

From April 1941 Home Guard members were required to pass a series of Proficiency Tests in the range of weapons they would be required to use in the event of invasion. Cloth proficiency badges were worn on battledress, but at least one battalion, the **24th Staffordshire (Tettenhall) Bn** issued a lapel badge **(N23)** signifying successful completion of the tests. The inclusion of the letters SS on the badge indicates its affiliation to the South Staffordshire Regiment.

The Home Guard was also raised in Northern Ireland, originally as an auxiliary force to the Royal Ulster Constabulary, and it was not until 1942 that the LDV in Ulster was renamed the **Ulster Home Guard**. By March 1944, the UHG totalled 24 battalions with a strength of 30,000 men. Only one pattern of lapel badge **(N24)** has been noted for this force so far, although versions exist with both gilt and white metal surrounds.

The spirit of comradeship engendered by the Home Guard was one that many in all walks of life were anxious to retain. Old comrades clubs were soon formed and from stand-down numerous **Home Guard Rifle Clubs** were formed. A lapel from an unidentified club is illustrated **(N25)**.

Auxiliary Units

Of all the tasks performed by the Home Guard, that which received least attention was undertaken by the members of the **Auxiliary Units**. This nondescript title concealed the fact that their job, had Britain been invaded, was to allow themselves to be overrun by the invading forces and become the nucleus of an armed British Resistance movement operating behind the enemy lines. Technically there were not members of the Home Guard, but they ultimately wore its uniform, being gathered for administrative purposes into three Home Guard Battalions, numbered 201, 202 and 203, these numbers appearing on their Home Guard uniforms.

It would have made little sense to compromise security by the issue of a lapel badge in wartime, but after the war a commemorative badge **(N26)** was issued. Shield-shaped and divided horizontally into red and blue sections, it bears the numbers of the three battalions arranged in a cross. It is unlikely that this was an official issue and its use may have been restricted.

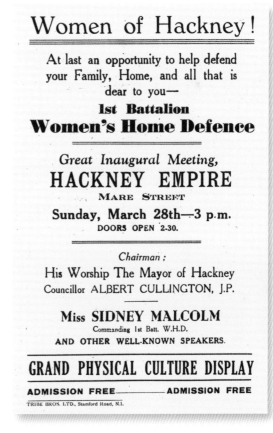

Women of Hackney!

At last an opportunity to help defend your Family, Home, and all that is dear to you—

1st Battalion

Women's Home Defence

Great Inaugural Meeting,

HACKNEY EMPIRE

MARE STREET

Sunday, March 28th—3 p.m.

DOORS OPEN 2.30.

Chairman:

His Worship The Mayor of Hackney
Councillor ALBERT CULLINGTON, J.P.

Miss SIDNEY MALCOLM

Commanding 1st Batt. W.H.D.

AND OTHER WELL-KNOWN SPEAKERS.

GRAND PHYSICAL CULTURE DISPLAY

ADMISSION FREE———————ADMISSION FREE

TRIBE BROS. LTD., Stamford Road, N.1.

Women in the Home Guard

From its creation there was agitation for women to join the Home Guard on equal terms with men. Throughout the war many units thrived with women acting as clerical or catering staff, but it was not until April 1943 that they were officially allowed to join the Home Guard, although still only in a non-combatant role. Initially designated as 'nominated women' they were retitled **Home Guard Auxiliaries** in July 1944. Total membership on stand down in November 1944 exceeded 30,000.

No uniform was issued although several units designed their own and some acquired battledress for female members. The official recognition mark was a brooch badge **(N27)** in a plastic material, issued from July 1943. It was supposed to be worn on the left side of the coat or dress, but as usual numerous variations are recorded. In units that had uniforms it was frequently worn as a headdress badge. A certificate was issued to all Home

Guard Auxiliaries making them recognised followers of the armed forces and therefore eligible for protection under the terms of the Geneva Convention.

The unsuccessful clamour for women to serve in the Home Guard and to bear arms in defence of their country (a right always denied to Home Guard Auxiliaries), led in December 1941 to the creation of an unofficial organisation founded by Dr Edith Summerskill, Labour MP for Fulham West. **Women's Home Defence** recruits learned weapon training and basic military skills, acting as unofficial members of HG units long before official recognition was achieved. Many subsequently became HG Auxiliaries when finally allowed to do so, one source claiming that ninety-five per cent of all members did so.

Uniform was actively discouraged by Dr Summerskill, the only distinction being an enamel shield-shaped badge **(N29)** in maroon and yellow, bearing a design of crossed rifles, a pistol and the initials "WHD". By July 1942 over 200 WHD units existed. The organisation stood down in December 1944 but continued in existence for some years as the **Women's Rifle Association**, members meeting regularly for rifle practice and competitions.

Invasion Defence

To many the threat of a German invasion of the United Kingdom is linked exclusively with the summer of 1940, but the possibility of an attack remained for several years thereafter. Government policy in 1940 embodied the principle of "Stay Put", ensuring that a mass movement of refugees, as seen in Belgium and France, did not occur here to hamper the military effort, but denying the population an active involvement in defending their homes. By 1942 the policy had become "Stand Firm". The duty of the citizen, as defined by the Home Secretary had become "to resist the invader by every means which ingenuity could devise or common sense suggest".

Following this belligerent statement, the Regional Commissioners put into place an Invasion Defence policy, under which positive action was to be taken by the civil population in the event of invasion. Local authorities set up **Invasion Defence Schemes**, building on the existing Civil Defence structure, to create a network of individuals preparing for active involvement in resisting invasion.

By this stage of the war there was little enthusiasm for new schemes, invasion seemed an unlikely prospect to most people and willing and able volunteers had long ago been snapped up by Civil Defence or the Home Guard. But at least one scheme produced a lapel badge. The grandly named **City of London Civic Guard** was created within the

Square Mile as part of this Invasion Defence organisation. Announced in October 1942, it boasted the Lord Mayor as Commandant. The Guard's aim was ill-defined, the City's Invasion Defence Officer being quoted as saying "it is difficult to define the exact nature of the duties they would be required to undertake in the event of invasion". Duties were simply to assist the military and CD forces in whatever way requested.

The Civic Guard's lapel **(N28)** featured the City's red and white shield below which appeared a title scroll. It is not known whether any other areas went to the extreme of producing similar badges. The scheme seems to have fallen into abeyance as the war progressed and the likelihood of invasion vanished.

In the years when our Country

was in mortal danger

PRIVATE CONDUIT   D. H.

who served   2 years   44 days.

gave generously of his time and

powers to make himself ready

for her defence by force of arms

and with his life if need be.

George R.I.

THE HOME GUARD

N1

N2

N3

N4

N5

N6

N7

N8

N9

If the Invader comes

N10

N11

N12

N13

N14

N15

N16

N17

N18

If the Invader comes

N19

N20

N21

N22

N23

N24

N25

N26

N27

N28   N29

LONDON REGION INVASION DEFENCE ORGANISATION

THIS IS TO CERTIFY THAT

MR ERIC CYRIL DAY

Full Name in BLOCK Letters.

National Registration Number

| BQDL | 52 | 4 |

has been appointed a

CIVIC GUARD

in the Invasion Defence Organisation of

THE CITY OF LONDON

Local Authority Area.

Invasion Defence Officer.

Date of Issue 7th January, 1943.

This slip must be surrendered to the Invasion Defence Officer on his demand or if the holder resigns, or leaves the area.

(C46622) 100,000 10/42

If the Invader comes

United against Axis tyranny

Overseas Forces' Welfare

Overseas Forces' Welfare

From the early summer of 1940, the United Kingdom played host to large numbers of overseas troops, many of whom could not return home to countries occupied by German forces. First to arrive from May 1940 were the Belgians, Dutch and French whose countries were overrun in the spring offensive. Later came Norwegians, Czechs and Poles, many of the latter having already escaped to fight alongside the French army after the fall of their country in September 1939.

Following the collapse of France and the Dunkirk evacuation there were some 20,000 French troops in Great Britain. On the 18th June General de Gaulle broadcast an appeal to all Frenchmen to fight under his leadership for the freedom of France. Of the 20,000 then in the UK, only 1,300 answered his call, the remainder being repatriated.

Two British-based organisations were quickly set up to look after the welfare of these troops, known initially as the Free French Forces. First to be established on 20th June 1940 were **Les Français de Grand Bretagne (Franco-British Liaison Committee)** an organisation, as the name suggests, set up by the French community in Britain. Their work involved extensive fund raising for the Free French and amongst other undertakings they presented fourteen unit standards to the Free French Forces on 14th July 1941. British citizens were eligible for enrolment as sympathiser members. The badge makers, Millers of Birmingham created two designs of membership badge for the Committee. The first **(P1)** was circular with the Union flag as a background. Superimposed on this was

the French tricolour and the words "Resurgam 1940". At top and bottom of the circle were two scrolls bearing the words "Les Français de/Grand-Bretagne". The second version of this badge **(P2)** appeared without the scrolls.

Alongside this organisation, whose aims were essentially political, were several British organisations which concerned themselves with the welfare of the troops. The largest of these, its membership predominantly British, was the **Association of Friends of the French Volunteers (Amis des Voluntaires Français - AVF)**, founded by the French HQ in London. Their efforts ranged from the support of rest and leave centres for the Free French to arranging the manufacture by British industry of French cigarettes.

Three lapels existed for the AVF. The first **(P3)** consisted simply of a round badge with a tricolour and the cross of Lorraine (the symbol of the Free French) in the white bar. The second badge **(P4)** was of similar design but having the letters A.V.F. below the cross. The third badge **(P5)** was of a completely different design, being circular with the tricolour at the top, the Union flag at the bottom, with the Cross of Lorraine in the white segment of the French flag and the letters "AVF" across the middle. The AVF also sold numerous fund-raising items, ranging from tie pins to brooches, on which the AVF symbol appears.

The number of Free French (renamed Fighting French in July 1942) in Great Britain was never extensive, although as has been noted above, they attracted a degree of visible support. In contrast, the largest number of exile troops, the Poles, (there were 17,000 by December 1940) seem to have left little evidence of similar activities. Perhaps due to the lack of a large pre-war resident Polish community in the UK, fund-raising or supporting organisations seem to have been few. A **Polish Armed Forces Comforts Fund** existed, but no lapels have been recorded, as seems to be the case with the popular **Scottish-Polish Society**, established in April 1941 in many Scottish towns . Organisations such as the uniformed **First Aid Nursing Yeomanry (FANY)**, provided canteen and welfare facilities, but again no lapels seem to have been generated. The author would be pleased to receive details of any Polish related lapel badges.

The situation is similar for the other European nations whose troops were based here from 1940. Few, if any, lapels were manufactured for the Czechs, Dutch, Norwegians or Belgians, possibly because of the relatively small size of the forces concerned. Illustrated are two badges **(P6 and P7)**, probably for fund-raising, for one nation whose troops were few in the UK, but whose plight seems to have attracted considerable attention. Greece, Britain's last ally on the European continent successfully resisted the invasion of Italian troops in October 1940, but was finally overwhelmed by German forces in June 1941. A government in exile was established in Egypt and armed services set up from volunteers and escapees. The plight of this nation seems to have attracted the attention of the fund-raisers, although little is known about the badges illustrated.

Not all the soldiers reaching this country were from occupied European nations. From December 1939, troops from the Dominions and Commonwealth began arriving to support the war effort. By February 1940 there were 23,000 Canadians in the UK, the advance guard of a force eventually to comprise five divisions. By the end of the war some 370,000 soldiers and nearly 130,000 other Canadian service personnel had passed through the UK. Service welfare of these Canadian troops was the province of similar religious and philanthropic organisations to those looking after the British troops (see page 154), and clubs and hostels were established at which off-duty troops could relax and find a touch of home. The best known of these was the London-based **Beaver Club** established in Spring Gardens near Trafalgar Square. Opened in February 1940 and supported by the Canadian High Commissioner, the Club offered a variety of services from haircuts and banking to Canadian style food. Staff were volunteers - mainly British women - who were provided with a splendid pin-back badge **(P8)** featuring a beaver and maple leaf on a red ground within a white metal circle. The date 1940 commemorated the year of establishment.

The impact of these earlier arrivals of overseas troops fades into insignificance against the impression made on the country by the largest force from overseas: the American troops who began to arrive in 1942. Under the laws of the United States, services' welfare was all provided by one organisation, the **American Red Cross (ARC)**.

Members of the ARC were uniformed, with distinctive insignia which is outside the scope of this book, but three badges are illustrated. Frequently mistaken for a lapel badge is the insignia worn on the peaked cap by all permanent female staff. This cap badge **(P9)** was an enamelled pin-back red cross bordered in white, each arm ⅞th inches long.

In some indoor uniforms this was pinned at the neck of the white blouse worn under the uniform jacket. It must be stressed though that this was primarily intended as a cap badge.

Two other lapel badges **(P10 and P11)** exist, although their exact significance has not been established. These are pin back badges, made by Fattorini of Birmingham. The central device in both is a red cross on a white ground. Around this is a coloured band with the wording "American Red Cross/Great Britain" in chrome lettering. Inner and outer bands on the badge are also of chrome. One has the coloured band in blue, the other in red. Given that American staff were uniformed, it is possible that these were issued to British volunteers who wore overalls when staffing canteens, but who would have liked to show evidence of their work when off duty. Many of the female volunteers in ARC clubs were members of the WVS who were entitled to wear the WVS badge (see L2) on their ARC issued overalls. In 1944, WVS Notes to Organisers mention, but do not describe, a badge to be issued by the ARC to volunteers who have completed 150 hours work in the clubs, "as a recognition of work done" and it is possible that this badge is one of those described above.

In addition there is a further badge **(P12)** incorporating the red cross on a white ground with beneath, a blue scroll on which are the words "World War II" and a central tablet with the letters "ARC". This is a post-war ARC badge issued to all members who had served overseas with the ARC in the Second World War.

P1

P2

P3

P4

P5

P6

P7

P8

P9

P10   P11   P12

THE BRITISH COMMONWEALTH AND ITS ALLIES
WILL DESTROY THE NAZI TYRANNY

United against Axis tyranny

Humanity keeps an appointment

The Red Cross and St John's

WAR ORGANISATION
OF THE
BRITISH RED CROSS SOCIETY
AND
ORDER OF ST JOHN OF JERUSALEM

Presented to

MRS. ARTHUR ALFRED STANBRIDGE

in recognition of devoted service to
the cause of humanity
during the second world war

1939~1945

George R.I.

Elizabeth R

Sovereign Head.
Order of St. John of Jerusalem.

President.
British Red Cross Society.

The Red Cross and St John's

Two uniformed organisations with distinguished histories played their part in the Second World War as they had in the First. **The British Red Cross Society** and the **St John's Ambulance Association and Brigade** were medical-based voluntary organisations whose function was to aid the sick and injured. The uniformed members, many of whom were responsible for the initial training of ARP first aid teams and the staffing of First Aid Posts, are outside the scope of this book, although two lapels for wear in civilian clothes **(Q1 and Q2)** are illustrated. Their administrative and fund-raising organisations however were widely represented with lapel badges.

In the First World War the two bodies had co-operated with each other and established a Joint Organisation to carry on their wartime work. In March 1939 a committee was established to look at the steps to be taken in any future national emergency and on 2nd September 1939 a new body styled the **War Organisation of the British Red Cross Society and Order of St John of Jerusalem** was formally set up. The activities of the body were to be concerned with "the sick and wounded of the fighting forces, prisoners of war interned in enemy and neutral countries and civilians injured or sick as a result of enemy action". No help was to be given to healthy members of the forces or the civil population, evacuees or normal hospital patients.

Only one lapel badge is known for the War Organisation **(Q4)**. Circular, it has the Red Cross on a white shield together with a white cross on a red shield encircled by a white and blue band on which appear the words "Red Cross and St John War Organisation", the whole surmounted by a crown. This was issued to a wide range of eligible people, from full-time workers at Headquarters who qualified after three months service, to full and part-time workers for County Committees employed in such efforts as working in convalescent homes or at parcel packing centres. Badges were to be returned once the wearer was no longer employed on War Organisation work and, if lost, were replaced if the worker put 1/- (5p) in a Red Cross collecting box.

On the outbreak of war in 1914, numerous groups of patriotic ladies had formed themselves into local work parties to produce essential medical and hospital supplies for the Red Cross. To avoid the confusion and waste that such uncoordinated effort had produced, it was suggested in March 1939 that the outlines of an organisation to oversee and manage such work parties in any future war should be formed. By August the **Central Hospital Supply Service (CHSS)** had been created to supervise the work of hospital supply depots and the production of medical supplies.

The Service embraced a headquarters, thirteen regional offices, supply depots and local work parties, all producing items to standard patterns sent out by the Society. The finished products were passed to military or civilian hospitals as well as a range of other recipients covered by the remit of the War Organisation. Over 5 million articles were manufactured from materials supplied by the Organisation and a further 3 million from materials supplied by the depots and work parties themselves. In addition 8 million items received as gifts from overseas were distributed by the depots.

A separate badge **(Q4)** was issued to members of the CHSS. Shield-shaped, it was divided vertically into white and black. In the white area appeared the Red Cross, in the black, the cross of St John. Below these were the letters "C.H.S.S.", whilst across the top of the shield was a red bar with the words "Red Cross and St John". Also shown is what is presumed to be an austerity version of this badge **(Q5)**. Circular with a tin back and edging, the design of the enamel badge is printed onto a blue paper background.

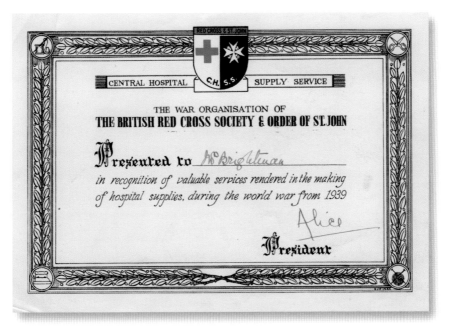

In Scotland, the BRCS retained a separate identity and amongst other non-uniformed activities, ran its own work parties. Members, operating under a branch committee set up on 20th September 1939, began production of comforts from January 1940 with a primary responsibility to the sick and wounded of the forces, but with authority to produce items for civilian air raid casualties. In the last year of the war alone, they produced over 800,000 dressings and bandages and 171,000 sewn garments. The Scottish work parties were disbanded in February 1946.

One badge is known, which has the appearance of a tie pin rather than a lapel badge **(Q6)**. It consists of a white enamel circle with a blue border on which appears the title "Scottish Branch British Red Cross Society". In the centre in gold letters are the words "War/Worker". The circle is mounted on a large brass pin which protrudes from both sides of the badge.

The greatest need of the two bodies was the finance to enable them to carry out their self-imposed tasks. In the First World War the Joint Organisation had raised in excess of twenty million pounds and it was felt that at least a similar amount was likely to be required in the Second. Fund-raising was carried out through the **Duke of Gloucester's Appeal for the Red Cross and St John Fund** which was publicly launched on 9th September 1939.

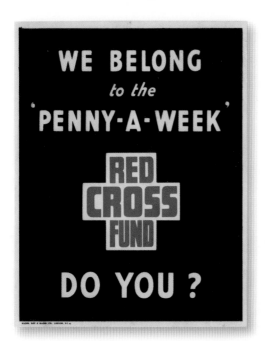

The fund's committee agreed that special appeals to particular sections of the community, combined with more general public campaigns were likely to produce the best results. In practice this resulted in a series of special appeals each of which produced one or more lapel badges.

The first of these, the **Penny-a-Week Fund**, alone raised over £20 million, one third of all the money contributed by donations. The principle of the fund was simple. It asked that each week one penny be deducted from the pay packet of participating workers and sent to the Red Cross. Initially aimed at those in heavy industry, it was gradually extended to smaller firms, banks, shops, the civil service and other organisations. Finally, through an extensive network of volunteer collectors, weekly house-to-house collections took place. Each level of local activity had a series of officials. A works representative looked after activities in factories and offices and local committees oversaw the work of the house-to-house collectors.

The scheme produced several badges of similar design, but so far it has not been possible to establish which badge was worn by which official. The design of the badge reflects the nature of the Joint Organisation with two shields bearing the Red Cross and the Cross of St John both surmounted by the crown. Around three sides of the design is a scroll with the words "Red/Penny-A-Week Fund/Cross".

There are three versions of the badge: brass **(Q7)**; white metal **(Q8)** and coloured enamels **(Q9)**. The last of these is almost certainly that worn by local committee members, the others probably by fund representatives in the workplace and by door-to-door collectors who, under the terms of the House to House Collections Act of 1940, had to wear an identifying badge whilst collecting.

Another source of funds for the War Organisation was found in the agricultural community, which during the war period accounted for some five per cent of the total British workforce. The organisation of the **Agriculture Fund** was based around the county committees of the National Farmers Union, with local committees below them. Activities organised included gift sales where items donated were sold for the fund, auctions of livestock, garden fetes, gymkhanas and horse shows. The Agriculture Fund also administered a counterpart to the Penny-a-Week Fund, known as the **Rural Pennies** collection. With contributors more widely scattered than in the town-based fund, collections from individual farm workers were co-ordinated on a village basis with over 85,000 village collectors for the scheme by 1944.

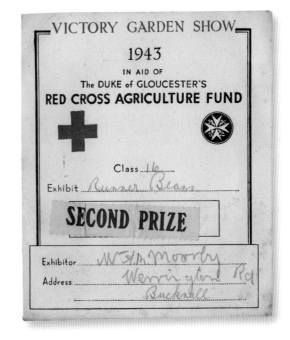

Three lapels are recorded for the Agriculture Fund, but again it is uncertain what each signifies. The largest, most elaborate design **(Q10)**, combines the two crosses within a blue enamel band surmounted by a crown and probably denotes a county committee member. The smaller badge with just a white cross **(Q11)**, was probably for junior officials. The third badge **(Q12)**, with its similarity to that of the Penny-a-Week Fund, is presumed to be for a collector for the Rural Pennies Scheme.

The official history of the War Organisation, published in 1949 (see Bibliography) mentions lapel badges for two other sections of the War Organisation, the **BRCS Appeal** and the **County Sales Section of the Appeal**, but it has not been possible positively to identify these badges.

Q1

Q2

Q3

Q4

Q5

Q6

Q7

Q8

Q9

Q10   Q11   Q12

For Men on Active Service

Service Welfare

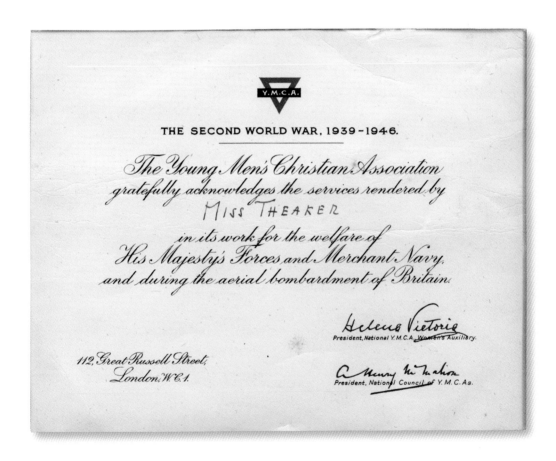

Service Welfare

In peacetime it was an officer's duty to look after the welfare of the men under his command. He got to know them as individuals and ensured that a man's domestic problems were attended to before they affected his ability to do his duty. In off-duty hours servicemen were provided with sports and leisure facilities within barracks and social and recreational facilities by organisations such as NAAFI. During the Second World War the management of the problems of service welfare grew beyond the abilities of individual officers and units. Most wartime soldiers were conscripted, leaving behind them more complex personal circumstances than peacetime volunteers, whilst the demand for recreation grew beyond the facilities provided by the pre-war organisations. In addition large numbers of troops in transit or stationed in newly-established camps well away from towns created further welfare problems.

The answer was found through an extensive collection of civilian voluntary organisations, many of whom produced lapel badges to identify their members. These organisations divided into two broad groups. The first consisted of the religious philanthropic bodies with a peacetime existence whose activities were significantly expanded to cope with wartime demands. The second were the local bodies which sprang up to service the needs of local men on war service or of servicemen stationed in their locality in war. In many cases these bodies restricted themselves to the provision of "comforts", - those small luxuries of life unobtainable from service sources including, until the imposition of clothes rationing, such things as knitted jumpers and gloves. In some cases however they took on a much broader welfare role.

Philanthropic Bodies

In October 1939, to ensure co-ordination of effort, the philanthropic bodies were brought together by the War Office into a consultative organisation known as the **Council of Voluntary War Work (CVWW)**. Its membership was made up of representatives from:- The Catholic Women's League, The Church Army, The Church of Scotland, The Methodist and United Board Churches, The Salvation Army, Toc H, The Young Men's Christian Association (YMCA) and The Young Women's Christian Association (YWCA).

Throughout the war these organisations provided recreational facilities such as canteens and clubs in the UK and later abroad. From June 1940 the majority of full-time employees in the UK wore uniform. All members serving overseas were issued with a service type uniform, complying with the terms of the Geneva Convention for civilians accompanying military forces in theatres of war. The wearing of lapel badges was therefore restricted to voluntary helpers.

The largest of these bodies, the **Young Men's Christian Association (YMCA)** had been looking after the welfare of servicemen since the early days of the Volunteer Force at the end of the nineteenth century. Over 170,000 staff were concerned with welfare work in the war period, many serving with the 500 mobile tea cars which visited scattered service units throughout the country.

Staff in the cars and canteens came from the **National Women's Auxiliary of the YMCA** which had been formed in 1918 for women who believed in the Association's principles. By January 1942, over 60,000 women were engaged in this work. On duty they wore an Association uniform, but in civilian clothes they wore the brooch badge of the Association incorporating its familiar red triangle. This badge **(R1)**, two sizes of which exist, was also worn as a cap badge when in uniform.

During the First World War, the YMCA had issued an insignia known as the **Order of the Red Triangle** to all members of the Women's Auxiliary who had given outstanding

NOTHING....

YWCA

IN THE WESTERN DESERT— and in isolated camps and war factories in Britain—the Y.W.C.A. is often the only " oasis " where girls, fresh from home, can enjoy home comforts and that friendly, homelike atmosphere they need so much. And, even in a strange town, a girl can be almost as lonely as in the desert itself. **Everywhere,** more-and-more Huts and Clubs are urgently needed by more - and - more girls.

...BUT THE **Y.W.C.A.**

Another £250,000 needed this Year

Please send as much as you can, as soon as you can, to: **Mrs. CHURCHILL, C.B.E.** (President Y.W.C.A. War Time Fund) **10 Downing Street, London, S.W.1** (Please mark envelopes " Y.W.C.A.")

DURING FEBRUARY LONDON BOROUGHS ARE ORGANISING SPECIAL " WEEKS " for the LORD MAYOR'S Y.W.C.A. APPEAL

● ●

Regd. under War Charities Act, 1940

service. This was revived in 1941 for service in the Second War. The badge **(R2)** is similar to a medal, suspended from a black ribbon on which is worn one red enamel bar for each year of voluntary service.

The Young Women's Christian Association (YWCA) was a much smaller body with similar aims but as its name implies, catering for women. The majority of its workers were full-time and from 1940 were in uniform if operating alongside service units. Some part-time workers were employed and these wore the pin-back badge shown **(R3)**. Another badge is also illustrated **(R4)**, possibly a lapel badge for supporters rather than one with a specific wartime connection.

The **Church Army** was another of the peacetime bodies which embraced welfare work including canteens, for the forces. Its involvement began prior to the outbreak of war when it was asked to second some of its officers to the Militia for "evangelistic work". Welfare provision eventually embraced over 300 mobile canteens as well as mobile libraries, entertainment coaches and static canteens. Again the majority of members were uniformed, with the lapel badge shown **(R5)**, which featured the Army's distinctive shield-shaped badge, being worn on overalls and civilian clothes by voluntary helpers.

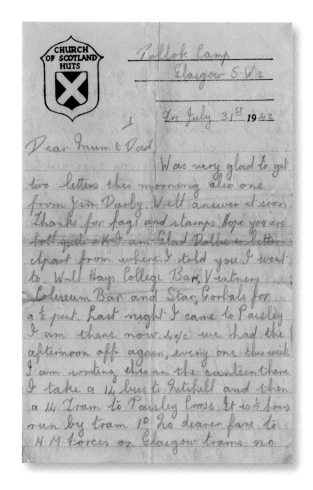

Four other badges from bodies within the CVWW are illustrated. The large badge from the **Church of Scotland Huts (R6)** appropriately incorporates the Cross of St Andrew. This records the revival of a concept from the First World War, of centres in which servicemen could relax when off duty, finding peace and quiet away from the noise of the barrack room or canteen. It is possible that in this size the device was actually a cap badge worn in uniform by members serving with the forces, whilst the smaller size **(R7)** may have been the lapel badge for voluntary workers. The badge

(R8), for the **Catholic Women's League** with its inscription "For War Service at Home" was again probably worn by volunteer workers, the title suggesting a form of service similar to that recorded on the National Service badges. The fourth badge **(R9)** is from the **Salvation Army**, whose activities stretched from station canteens to overseas rest and leave centres.

It was not only the established organisations which ran canteens or performed welfare work. Two other badges demonstrate the diversity of this field. They both include the word Welfare, one **(R10)** coupled with mention of HM Forces, the other **(R11)** in connection with Forces Canteens. Details of the origins of both are unknown.

Civil Defence Welfare

Welfare work was not confined to the armed forces. As the Civil Defence services expanded with staff remaining at their posts for long and arduous hours, they too began to need welfare provision. Mobile canteens were amongst these services and in London the **Metropolitan Borough of Wandsworth Civil Defence Canteens** marked volunteer service with the badge shown **(R12)**. Many local Civil Defence Comforts Funds (usually organised on a borough basis), existed under the terms of the War Charities Act of 1940 - for example the Civil Defence Comforts Fund, Bermondsey -, but so far few lapel badges have been recorded for these. The example illustrated **(R13)** from **The City of Leicester CD Welfare Service** suggests that some clearly had more wide-ranging tasks than the provision of comforts.

Service Comforts

The armed forces provided their troops the basic necessities of life. For luxuries, from warm clothing in severe weather to cigarettes, extra items of food, books, games, newspapers, musical instruments and sports kit, welfare bodies were the main providers.

From the outset of the war local bodies began to make woollen comforts for the troops as they had done in the earlier war. Anxious to co-ordinate this effort and to ensure the best use of scarce wool supplies, there was established a Joint Service Comforts Committee which kept the public informed of the types of garments most needed by the forces.

The campaign to encourage this co-ordination of effort was launched with an appeal to Lords Lieutenant, Lord Mayors, Lord Provosts and Mayors to establish local schemes in counties, cities and boroughs, registering work parties centrally and organising a depot to collect the finished work.

These continued to flourish throughout the war and a typical badge from **The Lord Mayor of Bradford's Services Comforts Fund (R14)** incorporates the city crest. The local crest again appears in the badge from the **Wood Green War Comforts Fund (R15)**, whilst the joint **Northumberland and Durham War Needs Fund** badge **(R16)** features symbols of the armed forces supported.

Much of the effort of these funds was directed solely to the knitting of woollen comforts and the role of the voluntary knitter is recognised in the lapels for the **Nottinghamshire Services Comforts Fund (R17)** and the unidentified mayor's fund, whose badge **(R18)** incorporates the V for Victory symbol (see page 193). Many funds did not restrict their activities to knitting and subsequently widened their scope to include welfare activities for all troops stationed in their areas.

In June 1940 the Chairman of the Joint Services Committee approached the War Office with a request that **Voluntary Workers for the Forces** not operating under the patronage of a local committee, might be issued with a badge similar to that used in the First World War. This had taken the form of the intertwined letters "VW" surmounted by a crown, all in bronze **(R19)**. These letters were to be included in a new badge, with a change in the materials used and the words "For the Forces" added. After discussion, the badge was approved in modified form **(R20)**, although the use of the crown was refused, as the War Office felt that the services needed to earn the badge "do not involve relatively onerous obligations". In its place the final version featured the lion of England set above a red enamel circle. Members did not qualify for the badge until they had completed three months work, and they had to purchase the badge themselves.

Army comforts did not all originate with the volunteers of the central committee work parties, who in any case restricted themselves to the provision of comforts to combatant troops at home and overseas. Much work was done through regimental or Corps funds, badges for two being illustrated. The design for the **Royal Army Service Corps Comforts Fund (R21)** incorporates the logo of the voluntary workers, but places it on a blue ground, replacing the lion with the Corps badge. Completely new problems with regard to comforts were created by the extensive employment of women in the army which followed the creation of the ATS in 1938. Many ATS subsequently served in very isolated locations such as anti-aircraft gunsites, where the need for any level of comforts was important. For them an **ATS Comforts Fund**, acting in place of a regimental fund, was sponsored from 1939 by the Duchess of Northumberland. Workers wore the badge shown **(R22)**.

Not all provision of comforts took place through the Joint Services committee. In some cases co-ordination of comfort provision for a single service was undertaken by one body – the **RAF Comforts Committee** being an example of this. Under the auspices of this Committee, working parties throughout the country completed their woollen comforts and forwarded them to the Committee's HQ in London's Berkeley Square for onward transmission to the RAF. Parties were recognised by the Committee if they had more than ten members although individuals could also qualify for the approved badge **(R23)** on payment of a shilling, if they completed and submitted four items. During the war 75,000 badges were issued.

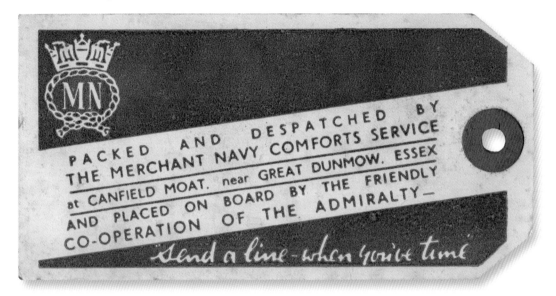

Comforts for the Royal Navy were administered by the Navy League, whose association with the Royal and Merchant navies dated back to the nineteenth century. It is interesting to note that the basic design of the badge **(R24)** for the **Navy League Comforts Supply** organisation is identical to that of the Admiralty contractors P.M.S.T. and Co. (see E11) Two organisations looked after comforts for the **Merchant Navy (MN)**, designs for both badges incorporating the naval style of crown. The badge for the **Merchant Navy Comforts Service** features the crown and two scrolls **(R25)**, whilst that for **B.S.A.S. War Comforts** (which may be from the British Ship Adoption Society) **(R26)** also includes the Merchant Navy badge introduced in 1940 (see page 220). Unfortunately, little is known of these organisations beyond the fact that they supplied MN comforts.

Service comforts in a variety of forms were also provided by many other organisations. Typical of these was the **Daily Sketch War Relief Fund**. The Daily Sketch, a London-based newspaper, set up a fund in 1908 (under the then title of the Daily Graphic Fund) to supply through the generosity of donors, food clothes and other necessities of life to the poor and needy. In September 1939 they extended this provision to those in the armed services and renamed it the Daily Sketch War Relief Fund. It undertook the same wide-ranging fund-raising and supply activities for the services through a network of voluntary workers, by collecting campaigns publicised in the pages of national and local newspapers and with collecting tins in pubs, hotels and the workplace. By 1941 the fund had supplied 3,800 wireless sets, 11,000 musical instruments and over one million knitted garments. Workers for the fund were eligible for the lapel shown **(R27)**, a chrome star with an heraldic lion at its centre and the fund title around an outer band.

Many servicemen wounded in action were returned to civilian hospitals for care, allowing a greater degree of help than might be the case if they had remained isolated in military establishments. Here again they became the centre of attention for the provision of the small luxuries of life to aid their speedy recovery. The blue and white enamel badge **(R28)**, records the work of a hospital supplies group providing service comforts.

Welfare of Prisoners of War

The nation's concern for its fighting men did not cease once they were captured by the enemy, although naturally the range of welfare activities which could be undertaken was limited. The Red Cross was the international body responsible for prisoners-of-war (POWs) and government work on soldiers' welfare and the provision of comfort parcels was co-ordinated by them. Workers on POW matters usually qualified for the badge of the Joint War Organisation or CHSS (see page 147). Other work was carried out by organisations similar to those providing comforts to active servicemen, often again at local or regimental level. Illustrated are badges from the **Leicestershire Prisoners of War Comforts Fund (R29)** and the Lancaster-based **King's Own Regiment Prisoners of War Comforts Committee**, the latter badge **(R30)** incorporating the regimental colours of orange and blue. The final badge **(R31)**, simply carrying the title **Prisoners of War Help** remains unidentified.

The trauma of a loved one becoming a prisoner-of-war, the difficulties involved in communications and the uncertain length of captivity, placed severe strains on families left behind. Relatives of captured servicemen were not the responsibility of the Red Cross although they frequently needed the support of workers trained in welfare tasks. This led to the creation in March 1942 of a limited company, (later to become a charity) supporting the families of POWs. **The British Prisoners of War Relatives' Association (POWRA)** was a subscription membership body with local branches throughout the United Kingdom. It undertook a range of tasks from organising Christmas parties for the children of those in captivity to issuing comforts to repatriated servicemen and parcels of such things as cigarettes to POWs. It also published a monthly paper with news and photographs from POW camps. On payment of 12 shillings (60p) annual subscription, members became eligible for the POWRA lapel badge shown **(R32)**. Other variations of this are recorded, including a version in brass with blue enamel.

R1

R3

R4

R2

R5

R6

R7

R8

R9

R10

R11

R12

R13

R14

R15

R16

R17

R18

R19

R20

R21

R22

R23

R24

R25

R26

R27

R28

R29

R30

R31

R32

Twice the number of human beings

Animals at War

Animals at War

The British are famed for their concern for and love of animals. It was therefore only natural that, faced with the threat of air raids, as much thought should be devoted to the welfare of animals as to the care and protection of the human population in the same circumstances. Prior to the war, at the suggestion of the ARP Department of the Home Office, the veterinary profession, working in conjunction with the Royal Society for the Prevention of Cruelty to Animals (RSPCA) and the People's Dispensary for Sick Animals (PDSA), established a **National Air Raid Precautions Animals Committee**, to ensure the well-being of domestic and working animals under war conditions. The Committee, usually known by its abbreviated title **NARPAC**, set up a national register of domestic pets and working animals together with a system of local representatives to implement it. Registered animals were identified by a numbered NARPAC disc affixed to a collar. This enabled animals separated from their owners to be returned quickly by matching the details on the collar disc to those on the register.

In October 1939 NARPAC received official recognition when the Minister of Home Security asked them to put into operation an emergency scheme for dealing with animals under war conditions. Tasks included the care or destruction of abandoned, injured and panic-stricken animals, the aim being to take responsibility for such work away from local authorities. Councils were asked to lend anti-gas clothing to NARPAC and allow free passage to vehicles and personnel of the Committee, both being identified by their symbol, a red circle inside which a white cross was superimposed on a blue cross.

The local representative of NARPAC was the volunteer **Animal Guard (S1)** Predominantly women they were responsible for the welfare and registration of domestic pets in their local area, usually a few streets. In a sense they equated to the local Air Raid

Warden. **Chief Guards (S2)** were responsible for a larger area with several Animal Guards reporting to them. Above these were **District Organisers (S3)** and **District Veterinary Organisers (S4)**. For working animals, such as horses, there was a separate **Animal Service (S5)** with **Animal Stewards (S6)** holding "officer" ranks. Controlling the whole organisation from a base in London's Gordon Square was a **Headquarters Staff (S7)**.

Members of the Committee were entitled to wear both an armband and a lapel badge. The lapels were in a standard form; a red enamel circle on which appeared the title, "National ARP Animals", the centre featuring the two crosses. Fixed below this was a curved bar with the designation or "rank" of the member. The majority are in silver coloured lettering on a white bar, except that of the Chief Guard **(S2)** where the bar is red and the lettering gold. When a government committee assessed eligibility for medals at the end of the war they noted that there were ten different variations of this badge but only nine have so far been positively identified.

Because bombing was not as severe as had been expected, NARPAC's services were less widely required than originally planned, although an estimated 600,000 animals were dealt with during the period of the major Blitz. The Committee ran into financial difficulties at the end of 1940 and the RSPCA withdrew its membership in July 1941. It was announced in December 1944 that NARPAC would cease to exist early in the new year and it was wound up on 4th January 1945, its assets passing to the PDSA. The animal registration scheme was continued for a period after the war as the National Register of Animals, and badges for this scheme are sometimes confused with those of NARPAC. An Animal Guard badge from the post-war period **(S7)** is illustrated.

In the First World War, before the widespread use of wireless for either civilian or military purposes, homing pigeons had been used extensively to carry messages over long distances. More than 100,000 pigeons served with the British forces between 1914 and 1918, but at the end of the war, military use of pigeons ceased. Shortly after September 1939 a new demand was raised for the services of pigeons, initially from the Royal Air Force whose aircraft were often forced down in the sea with no means of communication. By using homing pigeons downed aircrew in dinghies could relay messages back to their base. An urgent appeal therefore went out to civilian pigeon keepers who were subsequently enrolled as members of the **National Pigeon Service.** Trained pigeons were lent by their owners for serving with the Army, Air Force and Home Guard as well as with Special Forces. In the last three and a half years of the war, 16,544 pigeons were dropped into occupied Europe in the hope that they might be found by members of the resistance and used to send messages back to the UK. Thirty-two pigeons were awarded the Dickin Medal, the equivalent of the Victoria Cross for animals.

The badge of the service is illustrated (S8), featuring a splendid bird against a sky blue ground with the service title on a dark blue border, the whole surmounted by a crown. Badges are numbered.

A.R.P. + A.R.P.
DOG OWNERS!
DON'T EXERCISE YOUR DOG FAR FROM HOME, FOR YOU CANNOT TAKE HIM INTO PUBLIC SHELTERS

DURING RAIDS

HOME IS BEST
IF ANY DISTANCE FROM HOME YOU ARE BOTH WELCOME HERE, BUT WE CAN ACCEPT NO RESPONSIBILTY

S1

S2

S3

S4

S5

S6

S7

S8

Twice the number of human beings

John Bull pulls in his belt

Food and Salvage

Food and Salvage

As the government continually stressed in wartime advertising campaigns, food was as much a "weapon" of war as guns, aeroplanes and ships. To implement plans for rationing of scarce commodities and to ensure the fair distribution of available food supplies, a Ministry of Food (MoF) was created at the outbreak of war. Ministry staff, as members of the Civil Service were not usually identified by a badge, but many volunteers working on schemes to ensure adequate food supplies or advising the public on healthy eating, were provided with some form of distinguishing mark.

Four MoF lapel badges received official recognition. Two of these originate in the aftermath of the Blitz raids in 1940-1941. Particularly in provincial centres such as Coventry and Plymouth, these had caused such disruption to normal patterns of shopping and feeding that special measures were required to ensure that food distribution and the ability to prepare and consume hot food were restored as soon as possible. In April 1941 the Ministry approved the formation of motorised relief columns of canteen vans, mobile kitchens and water tankers.

With the permission of Her Majesty the Queen, these were known as **Queen's Messenger Convoys**, and were painted in a distinctive blue and silver livery. Each convoy comprised twelve vehicles with fifty volunteer helpers. They were to travel to severely blitzed areas and feed the local population where water and gas had been cut off and food shops destroyed. Apart from a small team of male drivers who assisted with the heavy unloading, staff were drawn almost entirely from members of the WVS. Permanent teams travelled with the convoys but local staff were recruited on arrival at the destination. Female volunteers on the convoys were issued with a distinctive badge **(T1)** echoing the vehicle colour scheme and incorporating the QM device in silver on yellow which was flown as a flag on the vehicle roofs. These badges were highly prized by the WVS volunteers and were withdrawn when they no longer served with the convoys. Male staff were not originally eligible for the badges, but became so in June 1941.

The disruption caused by the Blitz raids also brought into being an administrative organisation to work alongside local traders and caterers. The aim was to restore food supplies in the local areas and to make arrangements for the provision of scarce commodities as quickly as possible, without regard to too much red tape. These Ministry staff were appointed **Emergency Food Officers**. As these arrangements were not put in place until after the main air attacks ceased in May 1941 the EFOs were not employed to any great extent. Their badge **(T2)** incoporates the King's crown, as befits government officials.

MINISTRY OF FOOD
LONDON S.W.1

This is the emblem of the Ministry of Food. It is the banner under which you, too, are fighting; helping to defeat the enemy's attempt to starve us out.

Through rationing, price control and other measures, the Ministry of Food sees that all get a fair share of essential foods at fair prices.

But nearly half of our food comes across the sea. The U-boats attack our food ships, and although most arrive safely, some are lost.

Now, here is *your* part in the fight for Victory. When a particular food is not available, cheerfully accept something else — home produced if possible. Keep loyally to the rationing regulations.

Above all — whether you are shopping, cooking or eating — remember "FOOD IS A MUNITION OF WAR. DON'T WASTE IT."

Woolton.
MINISTER OF FOOD

FOOD FACTS
Nº 22

Issued by The Ministry of Food

Other measures to husband valuable food resources after air raids included the **Traders Salvage Schemes** introduced in October 1942. These ensured that if food could be retrieved from damaged premises without demolition, then local traders secured stocks at the earliest opportunity and co-operated to make the best use of them. To enable scheme members to operate near the site of raid damage some means of identification was needed, and it is known that this included the issue of lapel badges, but so far, no designs have been recorded.

As the war progressed all food became scarce, and an ability to use it to the best advantage a major requirement for every housewife. The **Food Leader** scheme originated with the WVS in Birmingham, where the city's Director of Education became concerned in April 1942 that food education and advice was not reaching those who really needed it. By 1944 it had become a national scheme. Its aim was to provide a direct link between the MoF and the housewife. Food Leaders distributed Ministry leaflets, staffed advice centres and passed on to friends, neighbours and other housewives they met in food queues, the healthy eating and food saving hints found in the Food Leader's letter they received from the Ministry. They were distinguished by the lapel badge shown **(T3)**, the shopping basket symbolising the weapon of war they were using to defeat the enemy. By February 1945 there were 15,000 Food Leaders in the country, the majority being WVS members. The scheme was carried on for some time after the war to cope with the continued rationing of food.

The Ministry also issued a lapel badge to full time staff in **Food Advice Bureaux**, but details of this badge have not yet come to light.

John Bull pulls in his belt

The War of Austerity

Prior to the war, Britain imported significant amounts raw materials other than food. Under the highly dangerous circumstances of war with military supplies having priority, shipping space was at a premium and imports of almost everything were drastically restricted. Imports of newsprint for example dropped from 420,000 tons in 1939 to 66,000 by 1942. The lack of raw materials had as far as possible to be compensated for to ensure a certain standard of living. The answer was found in what we now know as recycling, but which in wartime was known as Salvage.

Campaigns to re-use materials were a feature of the war almost from its outset. As early as October 1939, MPs were suggesting the recycling of derelict motor cars, trophies from the First World War, tram lines and railings. During the summer of 1940 the Ministry of Aircraft Production appealed to the country's housewives for aluminium to make Spitfires (see page 183). From that date onwards all sorts of commodities were collected for recycling into war materials, from bones to make glue to rags to make paper. Extensive salvage efforts went on throughout the war, although by the end of 1942 salvage of domestic tin cans had ceased as the labour required to reprocess them exceeded their end value. But the overall effort was worthwhile. Over six million tons of salvage were collected in the war, with enough kitchen waste collected each month to feed 210,000 pigs.

Initial collections such as those for the Spitfires of 1940 were voluntary, but in July of that year the Ministry of Supply made it the duty of all local authorities with populations over 10,000 to organise efficient schemes for the salvage of a range of materials, including scrap metal. Later this obligation was extended to areas with populations over 5,000. With this requirement local authorities began to issue those authorised to collect or organise salvage with a lapel badge. In February 1942 the name **Salvage Steward** was chosen by the Ministry of Supply as a suitably official title for those involved in this work, and a national badge was devised.

Three types of official badge were issued. Of the same basic design - the letter S within a circle surmounted by a crown, they were manufactured in plastic. For part-time stewards appointed by local authorities the badge was red **(T4)**, for full-time employees of shops and offices the badge was blue, whilst full-time employees appointed by factories wore the badge in green. Some local authorities issued their own badge, the designs again coming from the fertile minds of the commercial designers. Typical are those from **Rowley Regis** in Staffordshire **(T5)**, a county Borough, possibly Nottingham, Northampton or Newport **(T6)**, and an unidentified area **(T7)**. It is tempting to speculate just how many people noticed the irony in the creation of any form of badge to be issued to someone whose task was to save materials. Children employed as **Junior Salvage Stewards**, were known as Cogs and worked under the supervision of the WVS (see page 116).

Throughout the war, many commodities were rationed in order to ensure a fair share for all. One commodity vital to the nation's war effort was never subject to this form of control, partly due to the difficulties of devising a means of rationing and partly because of the overtones of nationalisation seen by some politicians in any scheme. The consumption of fuel, whether produced from coal, gas or electricity, was the subject of

John Bull pulls in his belt

much debate and many propaganda campaigns in an effort to divert resources to vital war production. To ensure the best use of supplies a Ministry of Fuel and Power was created in June 1942. Its first action was to exhort householders to ration themselves to a fuel target, based on allowances for a house and its occupants. This effort was successful; by 1944 UK coal consumption was only three-quarters that of pre-war years.

Fuel consumption in commerce was much more difficult to control, and this lead to the sponsoring by the Ministry of the **Fuel Watcher** in industry. These members of a company's staff were authorised to save fuel by all means possible, from switching off lights in empty rooms to ensuring that heat did not escape through open doors. In January 1943 the scheme was extended to non-industrial concerns. Hotels, hospitals, restaurants, schools, offices, shops and cinemas were all asked to appoint Fuel Watchers. Once appointed, Fuel Watchers were entitled to an official badge obtainable from their Regional Coal Office. This blue badge **(T8)**, in the economy plastic of the period, is a simple circle on which are the words "Fuel Watcher", crossed by a horizontal bar with the words "Heat-Light-Power". The fixing is a simple vertical pin without a catch.

T1

T2

T3

T4

T5

T6

T7

T8

John Bull pulls in his belt

Back the Great Attack

The National Savings Movement

The National Savings Movement

Established in 1916 to encourage the lending of personal savings to the Government to finance the prosecution of the First World War, the National Savings Movement had remained in existence in peacetime and was in place at the outbreak of the later war to fulfil a similar function. During the Second World War, the **National Savings Movement** with its offshoot the **War Savings Campaign** fulfilled two purposes. It not only channelled the public's money into the funding of the war effort, but also swept up spare cash which might have otherwise been spent on scarce consumer goods, resulting in retail price inflation. The Movement operated through a network of 1,200 local committees which encouraged regular saving, usually through the purchase of small denomination stamps stuck onto a card, which later could be converted into savings certificates. Most of the contributions were obtained through house-to-house collections or from savings groups in the workplace or street.

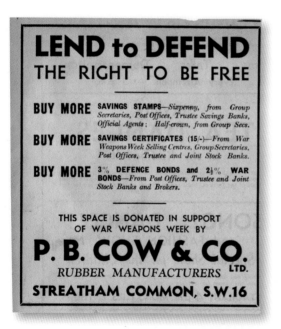

Until early 1939 one of the symbols used on both savings cards and lapel badges **(U1)** was the swastika, which in its reversed form had become the symbol of Germany's Nazi Party. It was felt that this was an inappropriate symbol for the wartime movement and a new design **(U2)**, based on the representation of St George killing the dragon which appeared on the sovereign coin of the period, was introduced. First used in the savings campaign of the war which began on 22nd November 1939, the image was combined with the ponderous rallying cry "Lend to defend the right to be free", this slogan subsequently being incorporated into much of the Committee's publicity. Two round lapels, one clearly an economy version of the other **(U3)**, feature both motto and St George. The badge served to distinguish savings committee members and local volunteer collectors.

In March 1940 permission was obtained from H.M. The King to incorporate the crown into a National Savings emblem, designed to give the movement a more distinct identity. This was subsequently used extensively on all forms of publicity from leaflets to flags.

From April 1942, as metal shortages made it impossible to continue the manufacture of the round badge, the new design appeared as a gilt coloured plastic badge **(U4)** to be worn by members of voluntary savings groups and committees. Consisting of the words "National/Savings" on two separate blocked lines which are mounted across a circle of laurel leaves, the whole is topped off by a crown. Only a plastic austerity version is known.

Throughout the war the local committees organised annual themed campaigns, with the public encouraged to reach target prices for individual weapons or equipment with their savings. For example they could raise enough to "purchase" an aeroplane or adopt a warship, their town or district name being displayed on it if they reached their target.

FIVE "SPITFIRES"

ARE WANTED FROM
THE BOROUGH OF WANDSWORTH

———

MAYOR'S FUND OPERATING IN:

**Putney (Roehampton and Southfields);
Wandsworth Central;   Balham and
Tooting;   Clapham and Streatham.**

The earliest of the themed campaigns, the **Spitfire Funds**, originated in the summer of 1940, not with the Savings movement, but as a result of publicity generated by the Ministry of Aircraft Production. Arbitrary prices for aircraft were published and local funds set up to "buy" them. In the summer of the Battle of Britain the Spitfire was the aircraft most in the public eye and any fund raising the sum of £5,000 was deemed to have purchased one. Once bought, an appropriate name suggested by the subscriber was painted on the aircraft. The County of Kent for example eventually bought twenty-two Spitfires - two of which were named *Gravesend Shrimp* and *Pride of Sheppey* - with the £108,000 collected by their local fund.

Lapels exist for Spitfire funds in two forms. Some are clearly those sold in return for a simple donation - the equivalent of a paper flag. Usually these include a representation of the aircraft, and most feature the area name **(U5,U6,U7)**. Some badges were produced in the shape of a Spitfire, sometimes marked with the town name **(U8,U9,U10)**. Others are more elaborate, either representing a significant contribution to the fund or perhaps being worn by local collectors. As with comforts appeals, some local funds were run under the direct auspices of the civic authorities as shown by the badges from **Bradford Lord Mayor's Spitfire Fund (U11)** and the **Cheadle Rural District Spitfire Fund (U12)**.

From late 1940, these annual themed weeks run by the War Savings Committees centred around displays of weapons or aircraft, usually with local parades and daily events to attract publicity for the campaign and encourage savers. The first of these, **War Weapons Week** took place between September 1940 and October 1941. Here the emphasis was on re-equipping the army after the disasters of 1940 although, as the badges show **(U14-U20)**, the designs included not only tanks, but also aircraft. The dates on the badges illustrate the way that the campaigns were staggered to allow the maximum use of resources.

No sooner had one campaign ended than another would begin somewhere else in the country. October 1941 saw the start of **Warship Weeks** where the navy took centre stage. Running until March 1942 most of the badge designs **(U21-U27)** featured a warship, the badge from Birmingham **(U26)** being an unusual exception by featuring the White Ensign of the Royal Navy. As with many wartime badges, the same design was often used in several places, as shown by the badges from Herefordshire in late 1941 **(U22)** and Hastings in the spring of 1942 **(U23)**.

In 1943 the theme was the air force in **Wings for Victory Week**. Badges for this campaign seem fewer than for the earlier ones, probably accounted for by the increasing

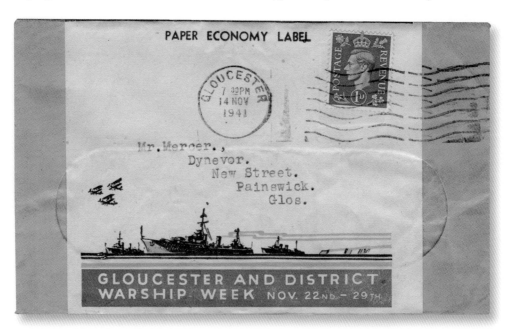

scarcity of resources available to manufacturers at this period of the war. The three badges illustrated **(U28-U30)** are all of paper, with a tin edging, demonstrating vividly the poor materials then available.

In the invasion year of 1944 it was the army's turn again in **Salute the Soldier Week**. Here one style of badge was available for all the local campaigns, with a space left below the main design for the addition of the town name **(U32,U33)** or with simply the year included **(U31)**. By supplying the badges centrally, the Movement was able to guarantee a reasonable standard of finish. Some local badges with poorer quality materials were still produced however, the design from Birmingham **(U34)** using again a paper centre within a tin frame.

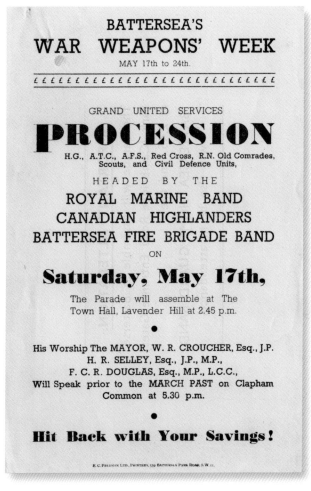

The ultimate campaign of the war, planned as a **Thanksgiving Week** for the early summer of 1945, did not finally take place until the autumn. No specific badges have so far been identified for this.

As in many other things, Northern Ireland did things differently. The **Ulster Savings Committee** operated similar fund-raising activities in the province. Their badge for collectors **(U35)** incorporated the red hand of Ulster on a blue map of the province.

Significant financial contributions were also obtained from the public to fund the work of the Red Cross. Details of their fund-raising activities can be found on page 148.

U1

U2

U3

U4

U5

U6

U7

U8

U9

U10

U11

U12

U13

U14

U15

U16

U17

U18

U19

U20

U21

U22

U23

U24

U25

U26

U27

U28

U29

U30

U31

U32

U33

U34

U35

Sing with ENSA !

Entertainment and the Media

FOR VICTORY !

Some Thoughts On the V Campaign by "Allan Junior"

Entertainment and the Media

In wartime, an opportunity to escape from the rigours of daily routine and be entertained was even more important than it had been in peacetime. What form this entertainment took was dependent on whether you were a civilian working in a war industry or a member of the services stationed somewhere in this country - perhaps miles from any major towns or entertainment centres.

The largest provider of mass entertainment, in both the home and workplace was the **British Broadcasting Corporation (BBC)**. Created in 1922, the BBC had a monopoly of radio - and from 1936 television - broadcasting in the UK. Television closed down on the outbreak of war, leaving radio as the main medium of mass entertainment and communication. By 1945 there were 9.7 million wireless sets in the country, one million more than in 1939, providing news, music and entertainment to the country in its blacked out homes, barracks and factories. Two channels, the Home and Forces Programmes broadcast daily from 7am until midnight. In addition, from 1940 the BBC became the only source of reliable information on the course of the war which was available to the occupied countries of Europe, severe penalties being meted out by the Germans to those found listening to the London broadcasts.

BBC staff wore their own lapel badge, fulfilling the function of the National Service badges worn by other commercial concerns (see page 57). This consisted of the BBC crest, as worn on the cap badge of the Corporation's uniformed commissionaires, fitted with a pin back. The badge **(V1)** depicted a twisted column from which emanate four lightning flashes, symbolic of wireless waves, together with a pair of wings, a reference to the wings of Ariel, messenger of the gods. In the centre of the badge in silver on blue, appeared the intertwined initials "BBC". Although almost certainly worn pre-war as a lapel badge, this was specifically described as the BBC's war service badge in contemporary accounts. There is an illustration of a BBC war correspondent in North West Europe in 1944 wearing this badge on a military beret, but it is not clear whether this is the lapel badge or the cap badge version.

In its role of providing news and information to the occupied countries of Europe, the Corporation was responsible for the creation of one of the most successful and best remembered propaganda campaigns of the whole war. In the spring of 1941, the head of the BBC's Belgian Service, Victor de Lavaleye, came up with the idea that as a symbol of resistance to the Germans in his country, the people of Belgium should mark the letter V on any prominent surface - signifying the word Victoire in French or Vrijheid in Flemish

- as a symbol of eventual Victory for the Allied cause. This was subsequently supported by the broadcasting of the opening bars of Beethoven's Fifth Symphony whose notes were those of the Morse code for V, three short notes (the dots) followed by one long note (a dash). This successful campaign was eventually copied in most of the occupied countries, the V-sign appearing on every available surface.

The **V for Victory** campaign quickly caught on in this country too. Lapel badges carrying the V-sign were produced and the symbol incorporated in any design containing the letter V. For the remainder of the war, the sign was used in innumerable ways to signify eventual Victory. It was also widely used in the United States, many of the items now available to collectors undoubtedly originating from there rather than the UK. Without a manufacturer's name on an item however it is impossible to be certain of its origins. Illustrated **(V2-V12)** is a small range of the many badges incorporating this symbol, ranging from the simple use of the letter and the Morse code representation **(V4,V5,V6)** through to the incorporation of the letter in the War Service badge of **Romac (V10)**.

During the First World War live entertainment of troops had become an important activity with many military units forming concert parties. In the inter-war years, the **Navy, Army and Air Forces Institutes** (NAAFI) had provided small-scale entertainments for troops in isolated camps. Aware that in a future war these activities were likely to be needed on a much larger scale, several prominent members of the theatrical profession met in 1938 to discuss how actors might be organised to provide a comprehensive national service in time of war. Originally conceived as an Actor's National Service Association, coverage was broadened to include all forms of entertainment, and in August 1939 the name **Entertainments National Service Association (ENSA)** was finally decided upon. In September 1939 it was announced that NAAFI was to be responsible for the organization, control and finance of the entertainments, with ENSA providing the actual entertainers through a series of committees. The first of many ENSA concerts was given on September 10th 1939 at Camberley in Surrey. Designed initially for the armed services, ENSA eventually provided entertainment for shelterers in the Underground and workers at munitions factories as well. ENSA was disbanded in June 1946, having continued in existence for a nearly a year after the end of the war to provide entertainment for the large numbers of troops in the occupation forces overseas.

Whilst serving abroad, ENSA members were required, from 1942, to wear a form of uniform (known as standard dress) enabling them to take advantage of the Geneva Convention provisions applying to civilians attached to the armed forces. At home the identifying mark of the ENSA artist was the lapel badge.

Sing with ENSA !

N.A.A.F.I.
PRESENTS
E.N.S.A. ENTERTAINMENTS FOR H.M.FORCES

In collaboration with **ENSA**

THE ROYAL CANADIAN
NAVY

PRESENTS

Meet the Navy

The Entire Production under the Supervision of
Capt. J. P. CONNOLLY,
M.C., R.C.N.V.R., Director of Special Services

Staged and Directed by
LOUIS SILVERS and LARRY CEBALLOS

SOUVENIR PROGRAMME

Four types exist - the basic design, by Sir Edwin Lutyens PRA, being similar in all cases. The badge is in the form of an inverted triangle, in the centre of which is a circle containing the letter "E". From this radiate three arms on which, clockwise, appear the initials "S", "A" and "N". This badge exists in plain white metal **(V13)**, bronze and in coloured enamels **(V14)** where the letter "E" and the outer border are in blue, the circle surrounding the "E" in red and the letters "NSA" in gilt on white. A variation of the badge **(V15)** has the letter "A" in gilt on blue above the "E" with a border in red. It is unclear whether this badge was worn by amateur performers attached to ENSA or whether it distinguished the Administrative staff of ENSA. The enamel badge could be worn as a cap badge in the standard dress, but it was usually replaced by the bronze version, as being less conspicuous. All three versions of the badge have been recorded as worn in the lapel.

Amateur entertainers did not all operate under the ENSA banner. In Bristol the Lord Mayor's War Services Council, responsible for a range of post-raid welfare services, set up the **Bristol Wartime Entertainers**. This panel of singers, pianists, violinists and conjurers provided a range of entertainments to Bristolians evacuated from the city to outlying camps or rest centres as a respite from raids. Established initially in the spring of 1941 when raids were at their fiercest, they continued their activities throughout the war. Their badge **(V16)** depicts a trumpeter in evening dress against a background of musical notes in black on gold. Around the edge of the badge, in gold on red are the words "Bristol War-Time/Entertainers".

In time of war, the distribution of news is usually controlled by the Government to ensure that information of use to an enemy does not reach them, whilst the news issued to the population at home portrays our war effort in the most positive light. In 1936 a subcommittee of the Committee of Imperial Defence suggested the creation in wartime of a **Ministry of Information** whose role would be to "present the national case to the public at home and abroad ... for the preparation and issue of national propaganda ... and for such control of information issued to the public as may be demanded by the needs of security". The Ministry was created on the outbreak of war and was finally dissolved in March 1946 to be replaced by the Central Office of Information, which at the time of writing still distributes government publicity material.

Two areas of the Ministry's work generated lapels although background details of both of them are scarce. The Ministry's **Emergency Information Committees** confined themselves to work after air raids, although had there been an invasion of the country it is likely that these committees would have played a much greater role than they actually did. The badge worn by committee members is described elsewhere (see page 108). Apart from a short period between October 1939 and April 1940 when it was the responsibility of the War Office, postal censorship remained a Ministry responsibility throughout the war. Illustrated **(V17)** is a badge with a censorship connection, the details of which have not been confirmed, either as to exactly who used it, nor when and where it was worn. It may indeed not even be a lapel badge, but it is commonly encountered as one, being pin-backed and much smaller than any military uniform badge.

The design consists of a rose, the traditional emblem of secrecy, within a wreath of laurel and surmounted by a King's crown. Below the rose appears a scroll on which is a Greek motto, translated as "We Work in Silence". The use of the crown implies official recognition. Some sources suggest that this badge was worn by military officers employed at departure ports to ensure that units proceeding overseas did not take with them material of use to the enemy. Whether these officers worked in uniform or civilian clothes is unknown. Any further details on the use of this badge would be appreciated by the author.

Newspapers do not seem to have produced any war service badges, although companies such as **The Times** created badges for their ARP organisation. (see page 44). The badge of the Daily Sketch War Relief Fund is covered in the section on Service Welfare (see page 159). If serving with the forces abroad as accredited war correspondents, journalists were required to wear military-style uniform, but details of this are outside the scope of this book.

V1

V2

V3

V4

V5

V6

V7

V8

V9

V10

V11

V12

V13

V14

V15

V16

V17

Lend a hand on the Land

The Agricultural War Effort

Name..... Miss O. E. Geddes

No. 10358

You are now a member of the Women's Land Army.

You are pledged to hold yourself available for service on the land for the period of the war.

You have promised to abide by the conditions of training and employment of the Women's Land Army; its good name is in your hands.

You have made the home fields your battlefield. Your country relies on your loyalty and welcomes your help.

Signed..... C. Delvmal.
Honorary Director

Signed ada M Palmer
Chairman Committee

Date .25·9·39

I realise the national importance of the work which I have undertaken and I will serve well and faithfully.

Signed..... Olive E. Geddes

The Agricultural War Effort

Without the ability to grow the majority of its own food, the United Kingdom could not have survived the Second World War. Intensive farming methods and the use of all available land, much of it not cultivated for years, allowed valuable shipping space to be diverted to more pressing war needs. Agricultural workers accounted for some five per cent of the total work force in the United Kingdom in 1939, but many of these were members of the Reserve Forces or were eventually called up, resulting in a labour shortage. Following the example of the First World War, when an organisation of women had been set up in 1917 to work on the land, there was created before the war a **Women's Land Army (WLA)** in anticipation of this expected shortfall. Under the auspices of the Ministry of Agriculture, the WLA began recruiting in June 1939, member number one coming from Somerset. The Army was to be a trained mobile force sent wherever in the country there was a need for agricultural workers. In December 1939 the total number employed was only 4,544 but by 1943 this had risen to 76,000. The WLA remained in existence until November 1950.

From the outset, the WLA was a uniformed organisation and full details of their uniform are outside the scope of this book, but they produced several badges of the pin back type which are sometimes mistaken for lapel badges and these are covered here. Each girl on joining was issued with a WLA badge **(W1)**. No position was specified for this and it was worn both as a cap badge in the felt hat and as a pin-on badge on the uniform green jumper. The design consisted of a sheaf of wheat on a green circular background, around which was a brass circlet with the words "Women's Land Army", the whole surmounted by a crown with the cushion in red enamel. These were produced by several manufacturers, and some are noticeably inferior in their construction. Issue of this badge was discontinued after 1942 due to the metal shortage. No other badge was originally issued, long service being indicated by a series of coloured armlets, but in 1949 the Army authorised a ten year service badge **(W2)**. This repeated the sheaf on the green ground in an ornamental oval shape, surrounded by gilt laurel leaves, the Army's title appearing at the bottom. A scroll at the top recorded the ten years service and the whole was topped off by a crown.

The WLA also created a Proficiency Badge to signify certain levels of competence in agricultural trades. Tests establishing eligibility for the badge included, milking and dairy work, general farm work, poultry, tractor driving, outside garden and glasshouse work, fruit work and pest destruction. The badge was announced in 1943, 25,000 being manufactured in the economy grey plastic of the later war period. It consisted of an eight pointed star **(W3)**, the top point replaced by a King's crown. In the centre was a circle containing the WLA wheatsheaf. On this circle appeared the words "Proficiency/WLA". It is not known where on the uniform this badge was worn.

In the summer of 1940 in areas such as Kent, many WLA members continued their work whilst the Battle of Britain raged above them. Machine-gunning of workers and livestock was not uncommon and the jettisoning of bombs by aircraft escaping pursuing fighters was frequent. When the George Medal was instituted in late 1940, the County War Agricultural Committee submitted details of several WLA members for awards, but all were turned down. Undaunted, they decided to issue their own bravery award to members who had completed six months work in dangerous areas and who were recommended by the farmers for whom they worked. Initially this was to be a cloth badge, but when samples of this looked disappointing, metal prototypes were requested.

Eventually a design from Miller of Birmingham was made up into an initial order of fifty badges. This **WLA Kent Conspicuous Conduct Badge** was subsequently awarded to nine members of the Land Army in the county, presentation taking place at a rally in Maidstone Zoo Park in July 1941. War conditions in the county never again approached the severity of the Blitz period and only two further awards are believed to have been made, these being presented in Maidstone in December 1942, making it somewhat scarce. The badge **(W4)** incorporates the white horse of Kent on a shield-shaped red ground below which is a scroll with the county's motto "Invicta". Below the shield is a curved bar on which appear the letters "KWLA".

Two other badges with a possible WLA connection have been recorded, but their exact meaning is not known. The first consists of a white enamel circle on which is a red St Andrew's Cross **(W5)**. In three arms of the cross appear the letters "WLA" whilst in the fourth there is a red diamond similar to that which appears on the WLA armlet. Further details are sought. The second item is a tin-backed badge **(W6)** originating in Winchcombe in Gloucestershire. Circular, it consists of a white ground with a central green circle. On this in white are the letters "W.L.F." Around the edge are two further green bands, inside which in black letters appears the designation "Winchcombe W.L.A.". Again, further details and the meaning of the initials are sought.

Even with the assistance of the WLA the supply of agricultural labour remained acute throughout the war. Use was made of troops and from 1941, enemy prisoners of war, initially Italians and later Germans. In addition, from the summer of 1942 there were annual campaigns to encourage civilians and school children to take working holidays on farms under the **Lend a Hand on the Land** campaign. The volunteer labour force in this scheme was organised by the County War Agricultural Committees who allocated workers to farms, organised their transport to and from work and administered the camps in which they lived. In the summer of 1943, 90,000 volunteers assisted with the harvest. Illustrated **(W7,W8)** are two tin badges from this campaign. Both contain the campaign title, one including the letters "VAC" for Volunteer Agricultural Camp.

Also illustrated is what may have been the equivalent of a War Service badge for agricultural workers in Gloucestershire. This consists of a green shield, shaped something like a farmhouse loaf of bread, with a horizontal bar protruding from each side. On the shield appears a stook of wheat, below which are the words "Local Land Worker/Gloucestershire/1942" in gilt lettering. This badge was probably issued by the County War Agricultural Committee.

W1

W2

W3

W4

W5

W6

W7

W8

W9

Citizenship through training

Youth Organisations

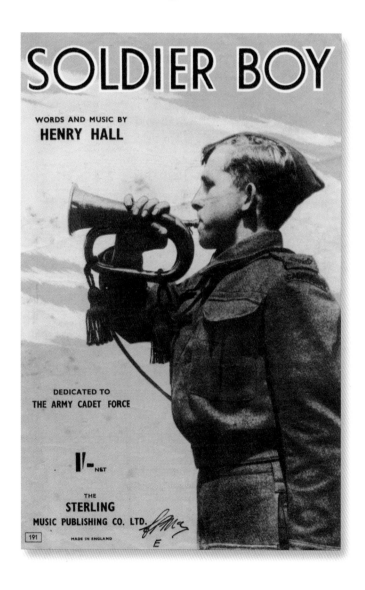

Youth Organisations

In November 1939, His Majesty the King wrote to the Prime Minister to congratulate the Government on its creation of a National Youth Committee, which, working through local youth bodies was to be set up to meet the welfare and training problems of young people. Subsequent to this, the Government issued an appeal for volunteers - especially those with previous experience of youth work - to come forward as youth leaders.

Organisations for Girls

One who responded vigorously to the national appeal was Miss Enid Walter, a former Board of Education inspector who established a Women's Air Cadet Corps along the lines of the Air Defence Cadet Corps (see page 210), with No 1 Squadron being based in Worthing. By February 1940 the Air Ministry had noticed its existence and promptly requested a change of title. The Corps agreed, changing its name to the **Womens Junior Air Corps (WJAC)** a month later. Its aim was to provide disciplined training and social events for girls from 14 to 17, later extending its activities to include pre-entry training for the women's services. Despite pleas that the Air Ministry had given it recognition, the Corps had no close connection with the Royal Air Force, the Ministry going so far, in September 1942, as to ban units of the RAF or ATC from parading with the WJAC. The Corps grew from 40 units in December 1941 to 212 units by May 1942, the majority in the north of England. Total strength of the Corps by this date was 20,000.

Both girls and female officers provided their own uniforms - initially a white or light blue blouse with tie and a blue or black skirt topped off by a grey field service cap - but later to include a grey jacket of ATS pattern and matching skirt. With the basic uniform members wore a cloth armlet embroidered with the Corps' device and a metal pin back badge. Triangular in shape, this incorporated a simplified monoplane fighter aeroplane, described in contemporary accounts as a Spitfire, but more closely resembling a modern glider. The cost of the badge was 1/10d (9p). This was worn both as a cap badge in the FS cap and as a tie pin. Two types exist, one in all white metal **(X1)**, the other **(X2)** in coloured enamels. It is believed that the more elaborate version was worn by officers.

In August 1942 the Government issued an instruction that no further companies of the WJAC were to be raised although established units could remain in existence. This resulted from a decision by the Board of Education, who were responsible for youth welfare, to form a co-ordinating body overseeing all training corps for girls. By this date several corps apart from the WJAC had sprung up, the largest by far, with 799 units, being the **Girls Training Corps (GTC)**.

The origins of this are somewhat confused. In the late summer of 1941 two members of the Mechanised Transport Corps (a uniformed body of ladies acting as drivers for government departments), - Mrs Mocatta and Miss Synge - had set up an organisation under this name to train girls for wartime service. Units were either centred in London Boroughs - No 1 Company GTC being in Croydon - or in girls' boarding schools such as Cheltenham Ladies' College. A number of these units were subsequently started as private initiatives and not as part of the MTC, although all seem to have taken the GTC title.

The Board of Education felt that the MTC, with its ATS style uniform and somewhat old fashioned outlook was too militaristic to run the Corps on a national basis, but it was at the same time anxious not to start another government-assisted body to perform the same work. It chose instead to sponsor a co-ordinating body, the National Association of Girls Training Corps (NAGTC) on which both the GTC and WJAC were to be represented. Its price for this co-ordination was that from August 1942 any new units raised were to be known only as GTC companies, although existing units could keep their older titles. The Corps was uniformed, girls providing their own outfits. Skirt, blouse and tie with an

FS cap were the norm, although there was a dark blue jacket for officers. Four types of pin back badge exist, all as far as is known, worn as cap badges. All incorporate the letters GTC within a truncated lozenge. A plain white metal version was worn by cadets, with two versions in coloured enamels for officers and NCOs (**X3, X4**). It has not been possible

Citizenship through training

to establish however which coloured background was worn by which rank. There are also much less common versions of the badge in all brass and bronze **(X5)**, but the significance of these versions is not known.

One result of the incorporation of the WJAC under the GTC banner was that many members of the former were not eligible for membership of the latter, whose lower recruiting age was 16. For them a **Junior Girls Training Corps (JGTC)** was set up with a variation of the GTC uniform being worn. Contemporary sources suggest that a special badge was created for these junior cadets, but no indication of design has yet come to light.

A further consequence of the reshaping of the GTC was the severing of the links with the MTC. Many adult members of the GTC had become associate members of the MTC to carry out these training duties. On transfer they retained the right to wear the badge of a **Mechanised Transport Corps Associate Member (X6)** with GTC uniform. This consisted of a smaller version of the MTC cap badge, crossed spanners on a motor tyre, on the lower arms of which were the letters AM. It has not been possible to establish where on the uniform this was worn.

There was a third constituent member of the NAGTC although so far no wartime badge for them has been uncovered. The **Girls Naval Training Corps (GNTC)** was formed in March 1942 by Commander C L A Woollard, a retired naval officer. Despite its title, like the WJAC it was neither approved of nor recognised by its apparent parent body, the Admiralty. Formed only four months before the creation of the NAGTC and the ban on further new companies except those of the GTC, it mustered only five units, mainly in south east London. This small size may explain the apparent lack of a lapel badge.

The GTC, WJAC and GNTC remained under the auspices of the National Association for the rest of the war, many girls from all three corps passing successfully into the women's services. But by late 1945 the two smaller corps were agitating for independence from the national body and the right to create new units. Before they could do so permission was required from the government departments most closely concerned. In August 1945 the Admiralty agreed to lift the ban on new units of the Girls Naval Training Corps provided that the name was changed to the Girls Nautical Training Corps. Units were happy to agree to this and the new GNTC became an established part of the post-war youth movement. No such change was required of the WJAC and from September 1945 they were free again to raise new units, doing so until at least the 1960s. Subsequent to these changes, the national association altered its title to the National Association of Training Corps for Girls.

It is interesting to note in passing that several other youth organisations sprang up along the lines of the three mentioned. Whether Tottenham's **Girls' Army Navy and Air Training Corps**, Dartford's **Girls' Emergency Administrative Service** or the **City of Bath Ladies Air Defence Cadet Corps** - all of which existed in 1942 - ever issued lapel badges may never be known.

Organisations for Boys

These new initiatives to prepare the young women of Britain for war service joined an already wide range of youth movements for boys and young men. One of the oldest and perhaps best known of these grew out of the experiences of its founder, Lt Col Robert Baden-Powell during the Boer war. At the siege of Mafeking he had employed boy messengers, teaching them the same principles of self-reliance and independent thought that he had previously taught to army scouts. In 1908 he founded the **Boy Scout** movement to develop these qualities of citizenship in all boys through training involving obedience, observation and self-discipline. By 1939 the Scouts had become a world-wide organisation with over three million members. The outbreak of war created ideal circumstances for Scouts to assist their fellow citizens and in common with all youth movements they quickly undertook a wide range of tasks for the Civil Defence services.

The Scouts were a uniformed organisation, their clothing in style and colour being modelled on that of the irregular cavalry or rough-riders of the Boer war. A National Service cloth badge, introduced in February 1939 was worn in uniform by scouts over 14 who could carry out a range of Civil Defence duties, but in November 1939 this was replaced by a Scouts' Civil Defence proficiency badge, also in cloth.

By 1942 the strength of the Scout movement was seriously depleted due to the call up of leaders, and they faced increasing competition from pre-service organisations such as the Army Cadet Force (see page 212). As a result the movement created War Service Scout Patrols to prepare members for eventual military service. Clothes rationing meant that uniforms for new members were difficult to obtain and non-Scouts who joined these patrols were authorised to wear ordinary clothes with a Scout War Service armlet and the Scout Tenderfoot badge **(X7)** in the lapel.

The Scouts also spawned the largest pre-war organisation for girls, recognised in 1910 and having the same aims of training for service. By 1939 there were 530,000 **Girl Guides** in the United Kingdom and one million world-wide, their name originating from the Indian Army Guides regiment. Pre-service training was eventually given to 16 to 18-year old Ranger Guides under the title of the **Home Emergency Service** but this is not believed to have originated any form of lapel.

The senior youth organisation for boys played a somewhat limited part in wartime, partly because of its religious origins. The **Boys Brigade** had been established in 1883 by Sir William A Smith and provided a range of activities which combined religious training and discipline. The basic unit of the Brigade was the Company, attached to a local church or similar religious body. Total strength in 1939 was 120,000 officers and boys.

Members wore Brigade caps and belts over civilian clothes and could qualify for a range of proficiency badges to wear with this simple uniform. In both the First and Second World Wars one of these was a National Service badge. The badge issued between 1939 and 1945 **(X8)** was awarded to boys who had rendered not less than 100 hours service to the community. Because of the nature of the Brigade's badges this is pin-backed and can be mistaken for a lapel. All Brigade proficiency badges were pinned in a standard order onto a cloth armlet. The National Service badge was worn on the right arm in the second row of proficiency badges. If qualified, it appeared between the bugler's and first aid badges.

There was also a lapel badge for the Brigade **(X9)**, designed in 1934 and worn by boys when out of uniform. This featured the Brigade's anchor emblem behind which appears a red cross with the letter B on each arm. A blue enamelled scroll with the title "The Boys Brigade" in brass letters appears below. Wartime economies dictated that only a non-enamelled version was available from 1941.

Every age produces new and exciting technologies which fire the imagination of the young. The First World War saw the rise of the aeroplane and, in spite of massive cuts in service aviation between the wars, civil aviation continued to develop. Amongst the greatest proponents of this new technology was the **Air League** (see page 222) which in an attempt to foster further interest, decided that it would establish a corps of air cadets to encourage young men to take up careers in civil aviation or join the RAF. A meeting at London's Mansion House in the spring of 1938 agreed to set up an **Air Defence Cadet Corps (ADCC)** and the first unit began recruiting in Leicester in July.

By 1941 there were 207 ADCC squadrons with 20,000 cadets, supported by an extensive network of local committees and businesses. The Corps was uniformed in a version of RAF service dress, but in civilian clothes wore a lapel badge. This **(X10)** consisted of a circle on which was the corps' title, inside which appeared in blue enamel the stylised "speedbird" emblem of the League.

As the war progressed the preparation of Britain's youth for admission to the armed forces was seen as an important role for the pre-service organisations and greater control of them was assumed by the service ministries. On the 1st February 1941 the creation of a much expanded corps was announced with the revised title of **Air Training Corps (ATC)**. The first local committees were set up in West Hartlepool and Whitley Bay and squadrons, with a maximum strength of 200 cadets, were soon established nation-wide. Over 1,000 were formed in the first few months with London setting up eighty-six. Existing

units of the ADCC were incorporated into the ATC, the letter F for Founding being included in the squadron designation to show their origin. The running of all aspects of the Corps was retained by the Air League until August 1942 when control passed to the Air Ministry. It was estimated that nearly 400,000 ATC cadets subsequently joined the wartime services.

Although there was no uniform for the first three months of its existence the corps was eventually uniformed along similar lines to the RAF, with a lapel badge **(X11)** available for civilian clothes. This featured a less stylised and more life-like bird than that worn by the ADCC, it being similar to that worn on the shoulder badge of RAF other ranks. Flying with wings outstretched it faces right and is encircled by a band with the Corps' title, the whole in white metal. An austerity version in grey plastic **(X12)** was also produced. There are also several varieties of the badge in coloured enamels, two of which **(X13, X14)** are illustrated.

Whilst the ATC represented to its cadets the challenge of new technologies, the older traditions of Britain as a seafaring nation were represented in a corps based around the sea. There had been a sea cadet corps in existence in 1856, but the Corps prominent

Citizenship through training

in the Second World War was initiated in 1899 when the **Navy League** set up a Boys Naval Brigade. By 1919 there were thirty-four separate brigades or units and on this basis the League applied to the Admiralty for official recognition. This was granted, subject to units being inspected annually by the Royal Navy. As a result the organisation became known as the **Navy League Sea Cadet Corps**, usually abbreviated to the **Sea Cadet Corps (SCC)**. The Corps' aim was to provide a seamanlike background for boys who desired to make the sea their career. Training included elementary seamanship, service technical matters, hygiene, physical training and citizenship. Like the ADCC, units were administered by local committees. In 1939 there were 100 SCC units with 9,000 cadets.

The outbreak of war in 1939 saw many SCC officers recalled to active service, but under the administration of the Navy League the Corps carried on, taking part with other service cadet organisations in the preparation of the youth of Britain for war, whilst carrying out a range of work for the ARP and medical services. In February 1942 the SCC came under the direct supervision of the Admiralty which set a target of 400 units with 50,000 cadets. The SCC is still in existence at the time of writing.

The lapel badge worn in civilian clothes **(X15)** features the naval anchor and crown and the League motto, all in white metal. There is a version of this badge in blue enamel with some details picked out in yellow metal, but this is believed to be a post-war pattern.

The largest of the cadet organisations belonged to the Army. In the 1850s the Volunteer Movement had begun to create cadet units to support them in their home defence role, either in schools or as open units affiliated to volunteer battalions. From 1910 with the creation of the Territorials, these youth bodies became known by the overall title, Army Cadet Force and once recognised, units were supported financially by the War Office. In 1921, following severe government expenditure cuts, War Office administration of cadets ceased, control passing to the Council of County Territorial Associations. In 1930 all government recognition of cadet units ceased. To compensate for this there was created a **British National Cadet Association (BNCA)** which took over the organisation of cadet units from the Territorial Council. By 1939 there were some 20,000 cadets administered by the BNCA.

The outbreak of war saw cadets involved in Civil Defence and other wartime activities and, from 1940, with the Home Guard. In January 1942, the War Office as part of the government's scheme to provide some form of pre-service training for all boys and girls between 16 and 18, regained control of the **Army Cadet Force (ACF)** although the

BNCA continued to deal with sport and welfare in the units. The ACF quickly expanded to over 180,000 all ranks and it was estimated that some 40,000 cadets passed into the army each year from its ranks. The force remains in existence at the time of writing.

Both adult officers and boys wore army uniform when on duty, but in civilian clothes could wear a lapel badge. Initially this was the badge of the BNCA **(X16)**, but in late 1943 an improved and more distinctive ACF design was introduced. This features the lion of England in an aggressive pose standing on its hind legs, enclosed within a circle bearing the ACF title, the whole surmounted by a crown. The first issue was an austerity version in brown plastic **(X17)** but an all brass version **(X18)** – possibly post-war – also exists.

Citizenship through training

X

Citizenship through training

X1

X2

X3

X4

X5

X6

X7

X8

X9

X10

X11

X12

X13

X14

X15

X16

X17

X18

Is your journey really necessary?

The Transport Industry

The Transport Industry

In an age when the private motor car is the most common form of transport, it is difficult to appreciate the reliance placed on more public means of transport during the Second World War. From the Merchant Navy, risking death at sea to bring food, raw materials and weapons to these shores, to the staff of the railways who moved these commodities - and millions of troops - across country to their ultimate destinations, transport played as important a part in the war effort as the armed services.

Railways

In 1939 Britain's railways carried 53.4 million passengers on Government service and 52 million tons of merchandise. By 1944 these totals had risen to 250 million and 87 million respectively, revealing clearly their significant contribution to the war effort.

The pre-war railway system was made up of four major railway companies and several small local lines. In September 1939 the Government set up a **Railway Executive Committee (REC)** to oversee the work of the railways in the service of the nation, in effect nationalising the railways. It also took control of the work of the **Railway Clearing House** which in peacetime adjusted the financial affairs of the railway companies to take account of the movement of passengers, freight and rolling stock between the companies. Their work and that of the REC was for the four major companies : The **Great Western Railway**, the **London and North Eastern Railway**, the **Southern Railway**, and the **London Midland and Scottish Railway**. In addition the REC also controlled **London Transport**, the **Mersey Railway Company**, **Kings Lynn Docks and Railway Company**, and the Light Railway companies of **Kent and East Sussex, East Kent** and **Shropshire and Montgomeryshire**.

During the First World War the railway companies had issued National Service type badges, originally only to men of military age, to indicate that they could not or should not enlist. The use of such badges was raised again shortly after the outbreak of war by the Railway Executive Committee, when it was reported to them that railway staff, unable to prove their identity, had experienced difficulty reaching their work during the air raid alerts of the first few days of the war. They requested permission from the Home Office to issue a badge similar to the First War pattern to include the crown, but use of this emblem was refused, in line with the government's policy of restricting the use of the crown on war service badges.

Eventually a new pattern was picked, with a common design for all companies. Oval in shape and made in brass there was at the top of each badge a steam passenger locomotive travelling to the viewer's left. In the centre was a blue enamel bar bearing upon it the words "Railway Service" in brass letters. Below this appeared the company initials. Examples from three of the main line companies are shown **(Y1-Y3)**. The badges were worn both in and out of railway uniform. Examples exist with a chromed surface, but it is not known if there is any significance to this or whether it is simply a finish applied by a local workshop to make the badge more attractive..

The following initials were used on the badges:-

Great Western Railway	GWR
London Midland and Scottish	LMS
London and North Eastern	LNER
Southern	SR
Railway Executive Committee	REC
Railway Clearing House	RCH
East Kent Light Railways	EKR
Kent and East Sussex Light Railway	K&ESR
Mersey Railway	MR
Shropshire and Montgomeryshire Light Railway	SMR

Badges were individually numbered the numbers combining with a letter prefix to identify the company issuing them.

The single exception to the standard design was the badge worn by the staff of London Transport (LT). In place of the locomotive, which would have been inappropriate for LT, there appeared the LT griffin, facing left. Below the bar the words "London/Transport" were given in full on two lines, the bottom word curving upwards to fit the shape of the badge.

Shipping

One of the main tasks of the railways was to carry from the ports the vast quantities of imported goods brought here in the ships of the **Merchant Navy (MN)**. Although MN officers wore either a standardised uniform or the uniform of the shipping line for which they worked, seamen of the merchant fleet wore civilian clothes both at work and on shore. To enhance their status and to identify the men to both sceptical civilians and dockside police, the Board of Trade issued a standard Merchant Navy lapel badge, fulfilling the role of a National Service badge, and according to the Ministry of Shipping in 1945, "recognised as a uniform".

The badges, 734,000 of which were made by the Royal Mint in 1939, were approved by the King on 9th September 1939 and issued from 1st January 1940 to all MN officers and men who signed on for a voyage in a merchant vessel after that date. Men disabled after 3rd September 1939 and unable to sign on again were also entitled to the badge. Issue of the badge was denoted in the seaman's discharge book (his record of voyages completed) by a rubber stamp which read "MN badge issued".

Also issued the badge were officers and men of the deep sea fishing fleets operating from British ports (subject to limitations on the size of the boats crewed) and from February 1940, subsequent to a complaint in Parliament, sea-going pilots. The first forty-one badges were presented by the Minister of Shipping on 29th December 1939 at the Dreadnought Seaman's Hospital in Greenwich, to seamen who had been torpedoed, mined or otherwise become unfit for duty since the start of the war. One recipient on this occasion was a woman, a P&O line stewardess.

Following the German occupation of Western Europe, men of many merchant navies served on ships of their own nationality trading from the United Kingdom. From December 1940 the MN badge was approved as an issue to personnel serving on ships of the Allied nations of Poland, Norway, Holland and Belgium. It could also be issued to seamen of Allied nationality - the Danes and Free French - serving on British ships. In November 1941, this provision was further extended to include Greeks and Yugoslavs.

The badge took the form of the initials MN surrounded by a rope circle knotted at the bottom, the whole surmounted by a naval crown. The official issue **(Y5)** was a pierced design in sterling silver, but an example with the ground behind the letters MN filled in with blue enamel **(Y6)**, probably a commercial version, is also illustrated. A file in the

Public Record Office notes that badges worn by Allied nationals were sometimes worn "with the national colours", but whether this means a cloth backing behind the badge or some form of enamelling is unclear. Commonwealth countries also used the badge: a version with a scroll bearing the word "Australia" below the main badge being worn by men engaged in Australia for service in vessels trading to any port in the

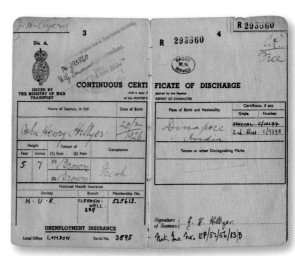

Empire. Issue of the badge ceased on 31st December 1946 following the revocation of the Essential Work (Merchant Navy) Order of 1942, which had effectively forbidden seamen from leaving the MN once they had joined it. The Ministry of Shipping agreed however that there was no prohibition on the wearing of the badge after this date.

Waterways

Britain's inland waterways were as vital a form of transport in wartime as railways. There is believed to be a national service badge for workers on the canals and other inland waterways, which consists of a blue grey badge about 25mm in diameter with the letters IW at its centre and the words "National Service" below, but no firm details or qualifications for issue have been unearthed.

Our three largest rivers, the Thames, Mersey and Clyde were all eventually patrolled by vessels of the **Royal Navy Auxiliary Patrol**, watching for mines and damage from enemy aircraft, but as a uniformed service they are outside the scope of this book. The same may also be said for the Port of London's **River Emergency Service (RES)**, a uniformed civil defence force operating on the Thames. No lapels are recorded for either of these services, although some form of badge for the RES was officially sanctioned in late 1939, which may possibly have been a lapel. A force similar to the RES which operated on the river Clyde did however produce a distinctive badge.

The **Clyde River Patrol**, set up in November 1939 received Admiralty approval to operate as a Civil Defence force in January 1940. It consisted of civilian volunteers under a Lieutenant Commander RNVR, carrying out the task of marking mines dropped in the river and the observation of shipping and dock installations to prevent sabotage. Unsuccessful attempts were made by the Royal Navy Patrol Service in 1941 and by the Home Guard in 1943 to take the patrol over, but it retained its independence until the end of the war. Some 1,300 people served in the patrol during the war. Active strength in January 1945 was 560. On duty volunteers wore blue overalls, a peaked cap and an armband all provided at their own expense, but off duty they sported the lapel badge **(Y7)** shown. It is similar in style to that authorised for the Special Constabulary and the War Reserve Police.

Roads

For many war workers their main method of transport to and from work was the bus. Operating companies saw passenger numbers expand out of all recognition as army camps and munitions factories sprang up in country areas not previously served by bus routes. Crossville Motor Services ran a fleet of 200 buses simply to serve a new Royal Ordnance Factory at Wrexham in north Wales, whilst the company operating from Salisbury eventually ran 119 buses daily to Blandford Camp on Salisbury Plain - more buses than its entire fleet possessed in 1939. Although the majority of drivers employed were men, almost all companies relied on women for their conductresses or "clippies". All the permanent operating staff wore uniform, but one wartime innovation generated a lapel badge.

Most buses were forced to carry well above their pre-war maximum number of passengers, especially at peak times. Very congested, movement of clippies up and down the bus to supervise the alighting and loading of passengers became a hideous if not impossible chore, delaying the bus. To overcome this problem bus companies recruited **Auxiliary Conductors** to their crews. These were regular bus passengers who remained on the bus platform throughout their daily journey to supervise the movement of their fellow passengers at bus stops, freeing the clippie from the necessity to return to the platform. These auxiliaries, originally unpaid, were eventually recognised by the Ministry of Labour and National Service as doing a valuable job and allowed wages for up to fifteen hours per week. As a mark of recognition they were issued with either an armband or a lapel badge. An example from **Stockport Corporation Transport (Y8)** with the badge number stamped on the face is shown

Air Transport

The early part of the twentieth century had seen the emergence of the aeroplane as a new form of transport. Its development was given impetus by the First World War and the years between the two wars saw the growth of civil aviation on both domestic and overseas routes. Details of the civil airline industry during the war are outside the scope of this book as the majority of employees wore uniform. The government, in discussing the issue of National Service badges for war work in November 1939, authorised the Secretary of State for Air to arrange for the issue of badges to members of the crews of civil aircraft actually engaged in flying, as it was felt that they ran the same risks as merchant seamen, but they insisted that the issue should not be made to ground staff. No further information has been traced on these badges and it is not known if this authority to issue was acted upon.

One of the driving forces behind publicity for this new industry had been the **Air League of the British Empire (The Air League)**. Established in 1909, this independent, non-political organisation maintained by public subscription, sought to spread a knowledge of flying and foster the development of British aviation. From its London headquarters, it published a monthly magazine, *Air Review*, keeping readers in touch with the latest developments. Members were entitled to purchase the lapel badge illustrated **(Y9)**, a stylised bird in flight, usually known as the speedbird, below which is a tablet with the League's name. This device was subsequently incorporated in the badge of the **Air**

Defence Cadet Corps (see page 210) which the League established in 1938 as a body to train young men with an interest in aviation for future service.

The League was also responsible for the creation in the 1930s of the **Civil Air Guard (CAG)**, an organisation for both men and women who wished to become familiar with aviation and who pledged themselves for immediate service in a national emergency arising from a war or a threat of war. The Corps consisted of units attached to light aeroplane flying clubs throughout the country under the central administration of a body of CAG commissioners.

From January 1939, CAG members were issued with a uniform of blue boiler suit and field service cap, wearing a lapel badge in civilian clothes. Two types are illustrated, both featuring the letters "CAG" in dark blue enamel. The first badge **(Y10)** is identical to the CAG pilots wings worn on the boiler suit and is believed to have been worn only by CAG pilots. The second **(Y11)** has the initials at the centre of a circular frosted chrome ground and is believed to have been issued to non-pilots. Many adult members of the CAG who were not eligible for war service, subsequently became instructors in the ADCC and ATC.

Established to make the best use of trained pilots was the **Air Transport Auxiliary (ATA)**. Created in 1939, the ATA was recruited from experienced civilian pilots with A flying licences who were too old or otherwise unfit for flying duties with the services. Set up by Gerald d'Erlanger, a director of British Airways, these pilots delivered all types of service aircraft, ranging from small trainers to four-engined giants such as the Lancaster, direct from the manufacturers to the RAF. By doing so, they saved the deployment of badly needed RAF aircrew. Total wartime strength of the ATA was 3,080 of whom 600 were pilots, approximately 100 of these being women. The remainder were concerned with administration and included maintenance and driving staff. For a short period in 1940 the ATA also recruited air gunners to protect aircraft on delivery from the attentions of the Luftwaffe. Over 300,000 aircraft were delivered by the ATA before disbandment in November 1945.

A dark blue air force-style uniform was worn by all staff on duty, but a lapel existed for off duty wear. A small oval pin-back badge **(Y12)**, this had at its centre a shield with the initials "ATA" in gold on white. Above this appears the head of a bird, its tail feathers protruding from below the shield. Its wings take the form of the flags of Great Britain and France. Across the bottom of the backing shield is a blue bar with, in gold lettering, the motto "*Unique et Ubique*" (Everything to Everywhere). No details of the use or origin of this badge are known.

Y1

Y2

Y3

Y5

Y6

Y7

Y8

Y9

Y10

Y11

Y12

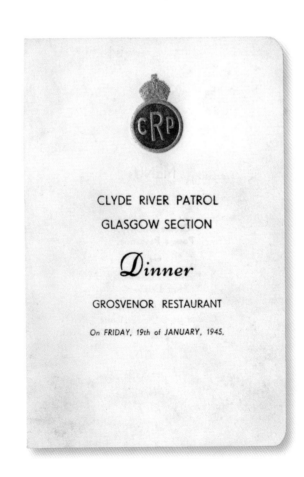

Carrying On

Recent Discoveries

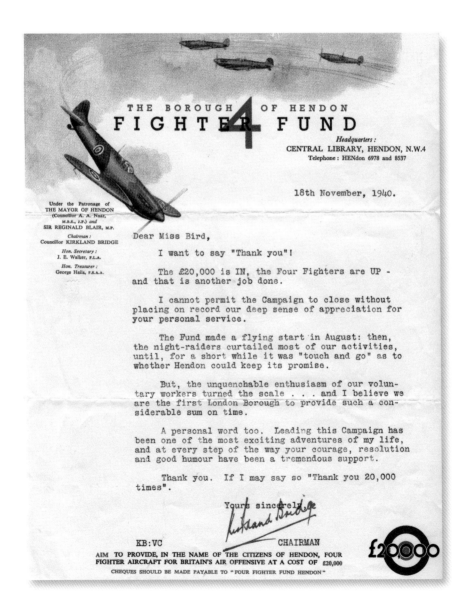

THE BOROUGH OF HENDON

FIGHT 4 R FUND

Headquarters:
CENTRAL LIBRARY, HENDON, N.W.4
Telephone: HENdon 6978 and 8537

Under the Patronage of
THE MAYOR OF HENDON
(Councillor A. A. Naar,
M.B.E., J.P.) and
SIR REGINALD BLAIR, M.P.

Chairman:
Councillor KIRKLAND BRIDGE

Hon. Secretary:
J. E. Walker, F.L.A.

Hon. Treasurer:
George Halls, F.S.A.A.

18th November, 1940.

Dear Miss Bird,

I want to say "Thank you"!

The £20,000 is IN, the Four Fighters are UP -
and that is another job done.

I cannot permit the Campaign to close without
placing on record our deep sense of appreciation for
your personal service.

The Fund made a flying start in August: then,
the night-raiders curtailed most of our activities,
until, for a short while it was "touch and go" as to
whether Hendon could keep its promise.

But, the unquenchable enthusiasm of our voluntary workers turned the scale . . . and I believe we
are the first London Borough to provide such a considerable sum on time.

A personal word too. Leading this Campaign has
been one of the most exciting adventures of my life,
and at every step of the way your courage, resolution
and good humour have been a tremendous support.

Thank you. If I may say so "Thank you 20,000
times".

Yours sincerely,

Kirkland Bridge

KB:VC ———— CHAIRMAN

£20,000

AIM TO PROVIDE, IN THE NAME OF THE CITIZENS OF HENDON, FOUR
FIGHTER AIRCRAFT FOR BRITAIN'S AIR OFFENSIVE AT A COST OF £20,000

CHEQUES SHOULD BE MADE PAYABLE TO "FOUR FIGHTER FUND HENDON"

A Twice a Citizen: *The Reserve Forces*

In September 1938 the Secretary of State for Air announced the creation of a **Civilian Wireless Reserve** to provide trained wireless operators for the RAF in time of war. Volunteers for the reserve were to be issued with a lapel badge **(A10)**. With the help of the Radio Society of Great Britain over 1300 volunteers had been recruited by February 1939. The reserve was absorbed by the RAFVR on the outbreak of war.

A10

The issue of badges for Army Reservists announced in 1939 **(A3 and A4)** was prevented by the outbreak of war. Not until October 1950 were the badges inscribed 'Regular Army Reserve of Officers' and 'Royal Army Reserve' sent by registered post to those entitled to receive them. When the Army Emergency Reserve was created in 1954 both badges were replaced by one with AER at its centre. The TA lapel badge **(A1)** was reintroduced in 1948 for both men and women.

B We must be Prepared: *ARP and Civil Defence*

Before war was declared the main job of Air Raid Wardens was to deliver, maintain and provide advice on the respirator or gas mask issued to every household. The initial distribution of these in 1938 required many extra staff, some wearing a badge **(B31)** to show they were officially employed on such duties. The badge issued to **CD Rescue Service Instructors** mentioned in the First Edition can now be shown **(B32)** as can a Bedfordshire badge similar to **B17** but with the more advanced ARPS qualification granted to instructors trained at the national **Air Raid Precautions Schools (B33)**. One of these schools, at Easingwold in North Yorkshire, produced a badge **(B34)** bearing the county's white rose; this may be a post-war item as Easingwold remained a CD and emergency planning college for many years after the war.

Like Liverpool **(B18)** both Manchester **(B35)** and Salford **(B36)** established Associations for their ARP Instructors. Badges similar to **B16** indicated the ranks of Birmingham's wardens by inscribing their centres 'Head Warden', 'Divisional Warden' and 'Senior Divisional Warden'. Salford also produced two variations of the badge for its Air Raid Wardens Corps with the city's arm at its centre, one with a red enamel surround and one with blue.

For the staff of the County's ARP Control Centre **(B37)**, Staffordshire issued a badge

B31

B32

B33

B34

B35

B36

B37

B38

B39

B40

B41

B42

B43

bearing their famous 'knot' with a more elaborate version for Sub-Controllers **(B38)**. Report Centre staff in another local authority Control Centre also wore a distinctive badge **(B39)**.**Hartlepool's Air Raid Precautions Officer** (ARPO), the professional adviser to the councillors controlling the Borough's ARP service, was issued with his own probably unique badge **(B40)**.

The badge produced for the **Reading ARP Rescue Service (B41)** is impressive although use of the crown, permitted on the ARP badge, was not officially sanctioned for other badges. Its size suggests it may also have been worn as a cap badge. The First Edition recorded no badges for shelter wardens like that issued by Plymouth City Council **(B42)**. Originally known as Shelter Marshals these were 'responsible persons, men or women with qualities of leadership' who, whilst unable to undertake the duties of a full-time warden, were willing to unlock local air raid shelters when air raid sirens sounded to 'assist in controlling the entrance and preserving order inside'. They were renamed Shelter Wardens in March 1941, from which date they were trained in the basic duties of Wardens and promised a uniform.

The nature of the air raids on Britain's cities meant long hours of duty without breaks for the ARP services. In such circumstances refreshments were welcome and ARP canteens, like that funded by the Socialists of Birmingham (**B43**) were gradually provided.

C Production must be maintained: *Industrial ARP*

Industrial ARP organisations probably produced more Home Front badges than any other service. They come in many varieties as many companies acted on Thomas Fattorini's suggestion and ordered the same badge with different coloured backgrounds indicating their different ARP services. In most cases it is no longer possible to establish which colour indicated which service. The examples here are from the **Co-Operative Wholesale Society (C63-C66)**, the **General Electric Company (C67-C68)** and the engineering company **Tangyes Ltd (C69-C70)** of Cornwall Works, Birmingham. The Cornish arms on the latter commemorate the origins of Richard Tangye who founded the company in the city in the 1850s. Many similar examples are known.

C63

C64

C65

C66

C67

C68

Carrying On

C69

C70

C71

C72

C73

C74

C75

C76

C77

C78

C79

C80

C81

C82

C83

C84

C85

C86

C87

Carrying On

Coloured backgrounds were often supplemented by fixing a metal label with the name of the ARP service below the main design **(C71-C73)**. **The Projectile & Engineering Company's** badge **(C37)** also exists with the scrolls 'Squad Leader' and 'Spotter' **(M10)**; that for the **British Oil and Cake Mills (C38)** with the scroll 'First Aid' **(C74)**. A design identical to that used by **Horrockses, Crewdson & Co Ltd**, cotton spinners of Preston **(C75-C77)** was also ordered by **Steel Peech and Tozer** who made steel in Sheffield.

The cost of badges to customers was reduced by varying a standard design for different companies. Variations of **C12** and **C34** in the First Edition are common; as well as the badges shown here **(C78-C87)** the design was used for the ARP services of Churchman's Cigarettes in Ipswich, Wm. Pearson & Co of Leeds, Liverpool Warehousing, James Beattie, Fisher & Ludlow, the Hartley Main Colliery, Wm. Parkes Forgemasters and Machine Products. Manchester-based electronic switchgear manufacturers Whipp & Bourne ordered a version with 'National Service' replacing ARP. MPM's Firewatcher badge **(F18)** also exists with ARP lettering. The badge for WD & HO Wills **(C79)** has been recorded with the colours reversed.

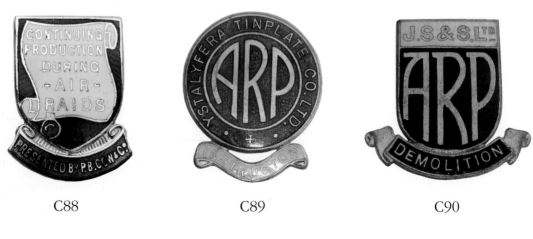

C88   C89   C90

C91   C92

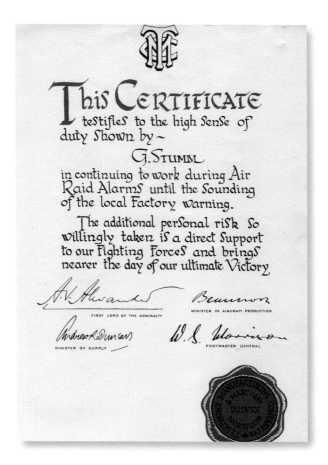

In the same way that local authority ARP services looked after the man and woman in the street, industrial ARP protected a company's workforce and equipment to ensure a quick return to normal production after raids – a necessity for companies engaged on essential war work. At least two badges were issued to staff who continued working under raid conditions. **C59** is now known to have been issued by **The Telephone Manufacturing Company** of Norwood, South London. In appreciation of work done 'in direct support of the Armed Services' each badge came with a certificate signed by the First Lord of the Admiralty, the Ministers of Aircraft Production and Supply and the Postmaster General. A similar badge **(C88)** was issued by **PB Cow Ltd**, rubber manufacturers of Streatham, whose 'Mae West' lifejackets and dinghies saved the lives of airmen forced to 'ditch' in the sea.

The majority of industrial ARP badges were issued to Fire, Anti-Gas, Decontamination and First Aid services but others denoted instructors **(C89)**, demolition squads **(C90)** and ARP Control staff **(C91)**. After raids it was important that damaged machinery was put back into operation as quickly as possible; **J Lyons & Co Ltd** the food manufacturers in London's Hammersmith issued their engineers a badge **(C92)** ensuring they were as easily recognised as other ARP personnel.

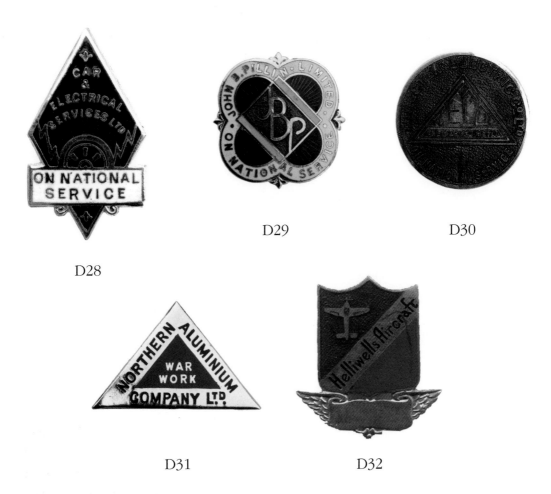

D28

D29

D30

D31

D32

D Have you chosen your job yet?: *National Service*

'On many occasions since hostilities started, various Ministers of the Crown have emphasised the importance of the 'Home Front' and openly acknowledged the work being done by Firms and Men engaged on Munitions, Supplies and in the various Utility Services. Many such firms are providing Special Badges for their men who are employed on these essential duties. They realise that the wearing of such badges is very popular with the men and their enthusiasm is enhanced, as it is their token of the important part they are playing in the country's effort.'

Judging from the large number of National Service badges recorded since the First Edition – one hundred in the last two years alone - many companies responded to this advertisement from Thomas Fattorini Ltd. The most common encountered wording is still 'On National Service' **(D28-D30)**, but others include 'Essential Work', 'War Production Worker', 'War Work' **(D31)**, 'On Vital War Work', 'War Worker', 'On Government Work', 'On Public Service' and 'On Aircraft Production'. Drums Ltd chose 'We Also Serve' whilst motor manufacturers Daimler chose 'Carry On'.

In 1941 Thomas Fattorini sent over 300 large firms a letter advertising a new range of badges. These were to 'serve as a permit whereby Gate-Keepers can easily see that only bona fide workers are admitted – a most important safeguard in works and services comprising Government work.' These badges have the company's name, sometimes with their logo and an area into which a works number corresponding to a factory pass or permit could be stamped. Some carry only the name and logo. Not yet stamped with a works number, the example **(D32)** comes from **Helliwells Ltd** 'of Walsall Airport and Dudley', manufacturers of windscreens, windows, nacelles, doors and seats for several major aircraft firms including **Hawker** whose famous Hurricane fighter they also repaired.

E The attack begins in the factory: *The Royal Ordnance Factories*

It is now known that 49 **Royal Ordnance Factories** existed during the Second World War. Numbers One and Two missing from the First Edition's list are now known to be the long-established factories at Woolwich and Enfield. Nottingham and Bishopton were numbers 23 and 32 respectively. To the original list ROFs 17 to 25, 31 to 38 and 51 to 66 can now be added. The news sheet illustrated in the First Edition came from ROF 53 at Bridgend. Badge **E6** has still not been linked with a particular ROF but to the original suggestions of Walsall and Wrexham can be added but ROF15 at Wigan and ROF 31 at Waltham Abbey. Wherever it was, it issued a further badge for Good Timekeeping using the crossed shells at its centre **(E13)**. Given the difficulties workers must have

Carrying On

E13   E14   E15

encountered in reaching their workplace in the ROFs which were extensive sites in isolated locations, a good timekeeping record was something to be proud of; ROF 57 at Kirkby near Liverpool produced a circular badge with 'Good Timekeeping Record' and '57' surrounding the letters 'ROF'. Examples with 'One Month' and 'Three Months' stamped below in black on a chrome tablet have been recorded. That examples of the 'Front Line Duty' crossed bombs badge have not yet been found in metal suggests it was never produced. The pressed plastic version **(E14)** has a safety pin sewn to the back to

ROYAL ORDNANCE FACTORY, KIRKBY

On the occasion of your leaving the Royal Ordnance Factory, Kirkby, I wish to express my thanks to you for the essential service you have rendered the country whilst employed here and to extend the good wishes of the Factory for your future well-being.

To _Miss E. Brady_

Date of Entry _20/10/41_

Date of Release _1/2/45_

Superintendent.

TELEGRAMS:
"ENTHUSIASM,"
BIRMINGHAM.

THIS BUSINESS WAS FOUNDED IN 1827
AND THE WELL KNOWN THOMAS FATTORINI PRODUCTIONS HAVE (DURING
SEVEN REIGNS) BEEN MANUFACTURED CONTINUOUSLY IN THIS COUNTRY
BY SUCCESSIVE GENERATIONS OF THE FATTORINI FAMILY.

TELEPHONE:
CENTRAL 1307-8
BIRMINGHAM.

THOMAS FATTORINI LTD.

REGENT STREET WORKS
BIRMINGHAM 1

MANUFACTURING
GOLDSMITHS AND
SILVERSMITHS

ARTICLES BEARING OUR
NAME OR INITIALS ARE
FULLY GUARANTEED

CONTRACTORS TO HIS MAJESTY'S GOVERNMENT

MEDALS - BADGES - CUPS - SHIELDS - TROPHIES - CASKETS - REGALIA

IN REPLY PLEASE QUOTE OUR REF. NSB/BU/6.   YOUR REF.   5th August, 1941

Dear Sir,
Identification of workpeople in Munition Factories.

    You probably saw recently in the press a question in the House
of Commons made to the Minister of Aircraft Production, that an
unauthorised person had been able to enter and spend many hours
walking about and looking at various processes at one of our
important Aeroplane factories. He entered according to report,
without challenge, and we are writing to suggest that if Badges
had been adopted for wear by all bona-fide workers that this
unauthorised person could not have gained admission, or if
he had got in he wouldn't have been there long without challenge.

    Some scheme of identification is compulsory by Government
instructions, but we claim that passes which are normally carried
in the pocket are inconvenient and very inefficient when compared
with a Badge which is worn on the coat and is thus readily seen
both on entering the works and at any other time.

    We have made many thousands of Badges for some of the most
important British Companies engaged on Government work, and could
make a special one for your Company if desired. Every Badge
should be numbered for identification purposes, and if you adopt
them we are certain you will find them much more convenient than
anything else for the purpose. Admission to the works with a Badge
is very much quicker than having a pass where a man has to get it
from his pocket, particularly in bad weather; it can be seen at a
glance as he passes the Time Office; a man can be challenged at any
moment during the day and asked the number of the Badge and his name
to see if he is the rightful owner of the Badge, and in this way
complete identity is safeguarded.

    If you have not yet adopted Badges, we shall be pleased
to submit a special design and quotation for your consideration.

    WE CANNOT AFFORD TO HAVE SPIES OR SABOTEURS WALKING ABOUT,
and the wearing of a Badge is a very great and definite safeguard
against such risk.

P.T.O.

LOOK FOR THOMAS IN OUR NAME AS SIMILAR FIRMS ARE NOT THE SAME

fasten it on clothing. Similarly marked to badge **E4** which was possibly issued by ROF 65 at Elstow, Bedfordshire is the PAD Service badge (**E15**). Passive Air Defence was the term used by the armed services for ARP and was a vital service in ROFs given the dangerous materials which they produced.

ROFs were not the sole suppliers of weapons and equipment to the armed forces, vehicle and aircraft production remaining in the hands of experienced civilian manufacturers. Two further badges have been recorded for the Austin Motors Shadow Factories which amongst other things built Lancaster bombers, the first similar to **E10** but with the colours reversed (**E16**), the second (**E17**) for their Shadow Aero Engine section. One of the most successful wartime aircraft was the slow and antiquated Fairey Swordfish torpedo bomber of the Royal Navy's Fleet Air Arm which, despite being effectively obsolete by 1939, remained in service for a further five years. Fleet Air Arm pilots flew it to cripple the steering gear of the German battleship Bismarck which enabled her to be sunk by pursuing ships. Production ceased in 1944 and that November the Ministry of Aircraft Production issued a 'Swordfish Badge' (**E18**) to all those involved in its manufacture; the first two were presented to the Prime Minister, Winston Churchill and Sir Stafford Cripps, Minister of Aircraft Production. A letter of thanks accompanied each badge.

Co-founded in 1931 by Nevil Shute Norway who, using his first two names, was a successful novelist, Portsmouth-based **Airspeed Ltd (E19)** produced two wooden aircraft which played a major part in the Second World War; 5,000 Oxford Trainers helped teach RAF aircrew to fly and their Horsa glider carried airborne troops to D Day and Arnhem. **Crossley Motors (E20)**, as well as manufacturing many of Britain's buses also produced vehicles for the RAF, including airfield fire tenders and the Queen Mary trailers used to move new or damaged aircraft by road. Airborne radar, a most valuable wartime innovation for the RAF, would not have been possible without radio valves manufactured by **AC Cossor (E21)** in north London. Typical of companies which adapted peacetime skills to wartime use, steel manufacturers **Newton Chambers (E22)** built 1,000 Churchill tanks at their works in Sheffield; in south London long-established leather manufacturers **Barrow, Hepburn and Gale (E23)** and their near neighbours **Blackburn Leather Goods Ltd (E24)** produced RAF flying suits and boots and webbing equipment for the army.

Continuous war production required maximum output from the machines of British industry. Anxious to ensure that valuable machine tools did not lie idle for lack of trained operators in late 1941 the Ministry of Supply asked the Machine Tool Trade Association to recruit volunteers for an **Emergency Machine Tool Armament Corps (E25)**. The 200 expert machine tool operators and demonstrators who volunteered for EMTAC were sent to factories to train new operators on underused machines.

E16

E17

E18

E19

E20

E21

E22

E23

E24

E25

Carrying On

F27

F28

F29

F30

F31

F32

F Fall in the fire bomb fighters: *The Fire Services*

The Civil Defence Act of 1939 placed an obligation on large businesses to train a percentage of their employees in fire fighting. Many large firms already had industrial fire brigades; with the company's winged shoe logo at its centre the badge from the **Goodyear Tyre and Rubber Company Ltd (F27)** in Wolverhampton suggests that their fire brigade also formed the basis of their ARP department. Others raised Auxiliary Fire Service (AFS) units similar to those supporting local fire brigades. A badge for the Auxiliary Fire Service of Glasgow shipbuilders Fairfield's was illustrated as **C54**; two more are shown here. The Avery badge **(F28)** was worn by the fire crews of **W&T Avery** of Soho Works, Birmingham, manufacturers of scales and weighing equipment, the crest with the 'Aux Fire' scroll **(F29)** remains unidentified. Strode's School, a boy's grammar in Egham, Surrey was unlikely to have had its own fire brigade but the wording on the badge **(F30)** suggests that senior pupils may have been trained to deal with incendiaries dropped on the school's premises.

Fire Watchers were vital to the safety of many factories; **Wilson & Co Barnsley Ltd**, bobbin manufacturers to the textile industry, supplied theirs with a badge **(F3)** with both coloured background and added scroll. An interesting aspect of the civilian war effort is represented by the **NFS Old Comrades** badge **(F32)** which commemorates the service of Column 4 of the **NFS Overseas Contingent**. Plans for the invasion of Europe in 1944 included National Fire Service volunteers serving alongside the armed forces to deal with any large fires in depots behind the front lines caused by enemy action or accidents. Five Overseas Columns, trained to operate alongside the army were formed, but only No 4 went overseas. Landing in January 1945 it served with the US and British armies before returning home in July 1946.

Form No. 161 F.

No. 2011

Rank W. A. P. C

Name Hulbert, Gwendoline. Alice.

is a member of the Wiltshire Women's Auxiliary Police Corps and is in the execution of her duty as such.

Noël Llewellyn

Lt. Col.,
Chief Constable and
County A.R.P. Controller.

Signature of holder

Hulbert.
Gwendoline. Alice.
G. A. Hulbert.

G In the Office of Constable: *The Police*

Special Constabulary lapel badges remain the most frequently encountered police badges, the majority having 'SC' on a blue ground separated by a coat of arms **(G4** and **G6)**; the badge for the **Special Constables of Kent (G19)** is slightly unusual in having a red ground. Twenty forces used initials similar to those shown on the badge of Luton's Specials **(G20)**; others include ASC, BSC, DSC, GSC, HSC, IWSC, LSC, P&K SC, RSC and

Carrying On

G19   G20   G21

G20

WSC all with a large 'S' at the centre. Two badges for the smaller **Police War Reserve in Manchester (G21)** and **First Police Reserve (G22)** are shown. Those for the WAPC and PAMS remain scarce; only one WAPC example has been recorded since the First Edition.

H   Especially suited to Women: *The Ambulance Service*

As the First Edition noted most Ambulance Services formed part of the CD Services and were uniformed. One further badge for Ambulance Services has been recorded since the First Edition; a white celluloid ground printed 'A.R.P./Aux./Ambulance Driver/N' in black block capitals. Nothing is known of its origins or the significance of the letter N.

J ...and not a single patient: *The Medical and Hospital Services*

The CNR badge with the additional letters 'NA' described in the First Edition can now be illustrated (**J10**). No firm identification of this badge is yet possible; records from May 1944 show that the only badge issued to the CNR was **J3**. It may have been issued to the Nursing Auxiliaries who remained with the CNR after the war. The two badges for **First Aid Posts** in Walsall (**J11**) and Bloxwich (**J12**) in Staffordshire both carry the white cross instead of the internationally recognised and protected red which was only used by the British Red Cross Society. The Hatherton Road Post was staffed throughout the war and published its own magazine.

J10   J11   J12

K If you are bombed out: *The Post-Raid Services*

Further badges for Rest Centre or Post-Raid Welfare Services including that for the County Borough of Tynemouth (**K15**) have been noted. A badge issued to Manchester's Rest Centre Service was identical in design to **K6** in the First Edition but with a blue ground and the Manchester coat of arms. The design of **K4** was also used by the neighbouring county of Holland in Lincolnshire with a change of coat of arms and county name. The City of Lincoln's Air Raid Welfare workers wore a gilt badge with the City's shield at its centre. Only one badge has been recorded for Scotland's Emergency Relief Organisation, a blue celluloid circle with 'E.R.O.' in white.

War Office records show that just over 400 companies and government factories had Auxiliary Bomb Disposal Units by 1943, ranging in size from the four men of Sperry Gyroscope in Gloucestershire to the 93 working at the Bridgend Royal Ordnance Factory.

K15   K16   K17

K18   K19

Four further badges are illustrated; the ABDU of **Accles and Pollock (K16)** who manufactured steel tubes in Oldbury, Birmingham had 35 men; the squad from **Machine Products (K17)** making radio equipment in Cardiff had 15 men, the **Bell Punch Company's** squad **(K18)** in London comprised 12 volunteers. The badge with '9' on the body of the bomb **(K19)** has not yet been linked with a company. ABDUs were graded A, B or C according to their standard of training and ability to deal with bombs. By 1943 only ten per cent of the 400 ABDUs were A-graded. The A on the bomb tail of the Machine Products' badge is believed to indicate their A grade status.

L The Ladies in green: *The Women's Voluntary Services*

The Women's Voluntary Services first came to the public's attention for their work with the evacuees at the outbreak of war. Local authorities in areas receiving evacuees

L10

L11

L12

L13

L14

L15

L16

L17

appointed key staff, usually from their education authorities, to ensure a smooth reception for those evacuated from the inner cities. The badge **(L10)** issued by an unidentified Rural District Council is the only Home Front badge so far found with a connection with evacuation as – cloth armbands seem to have been more common.

Whilst **L5** is the most commonly encountered style of badge for the **Housewives Service**, two others in contrasting styles are shown; the Exeter example in metal **(L11)** the Somerset **(L12)** in card similar to that produced for the adjoining city of Bristol **(L6)**.

A badge recorded for the Housewives Service in the village of Bushbury in Staffordshire has 'Bushbury Housewives Service' in gold on blue surrounding 'ARP' in red on a yellow ground. Further examples of the WVS brooch 'rank badges' listed in the First Edition are illustrated **(L13-L17)**.

M Forewarned is Forearmed: *The Royal Observer Corps*

The all-white metal version of the badge **(M3)** is now known to be the version issued by the RAF when the Air Ministry assumed responsibility for the Observer Corps on the outbreak of war. Both types of lapel badge were worn as unofficial headdress badges in the beret of male observers and the blue field service cap of women volunteers. The badge of the **National Association of Spotters Clubs (M6)**, described but not illustrated in the First Edition was also made as a water-slide transfer for application to the steel helmet. Before the introduction of the NASC badge the **Spotters' Club of Oldham** and District introduced their own badge **(M7)**, its design ingeniously combining binoculars and a pair of wings.

M6

M7

M8

M9

M10

Carrying On

Early air raids severely interrupted industrial production until companies placed trained spotters – Winston Churchill christened them 'Jim Crows' - on the roofs of their buildings whose job was to sound an alarm for their buildings only when there was an immediate threat from enemy air activity. WHARCO – **WH Robinson and Co** in Bedford who made machinery for steel plants - gave their spotters a simple celluloid, tin-backed badge **(M8)**. The more elaborate badge for spotters of **The Projectile and Engineering Company** of London SW8 **(M9)** was achieved by adding a 'Spotter' scroll to the badge issued to the company's other ARP services **(C37)**. **Kemsley House**, home of the Daily Sketch in London described their spotters **(M10)** as 'Roof Watchers''

N If the Invader comes: *The Home Guard and Invasion Defence*

The short life of the Local Defence Volunteers between 14th May and 23rd July 1940 left little time for the manufacture of LDV lapel badges. Only one further example has been recorded since the First Edition, a blue enamel circle with 'Bearsden' surrounding the letters 'LDV'. LDV volunteers from Bearsden, a suburb of Glasgow, later formed the 3rd Dumbartonshire Battalion of Scotland's Home Guard.

Units raised for the local defence of factories and vulnerable points were a feature of the early years of the Home Guard, the majority incorporated after 1941 into General Service battalions. Three further badges for these early units are illustrated; the volunteers defending the works of printers and engravers **John Meerloos & Co (N30)** in London's Mile End Road were almost certainly few in number compared with the large workforce available to the **General Electric Company (GEC)** in Birmingham **(N31)**. A similar circular badge was produced for **Metro-Cammell (N32)**, railway carriage and wagon manufacturers in the city. Both incorporate the antelope cap badge of the county

N30   N31   N32

regiment, the Royal Warwickshires which Home Guards were authorised to wear at the beginning of August 1940. The exact details of the third badge **(N33)** are unknown but it was probably issued by a Borough Gas Company (BGC); the 1940 edition of The Municipal Yearbook records twenty Municipal Boroughs with names starting with D who might have run their own gasworks. Several examples of the 'Home Guard' tablet used on **N9** have been recorded with a smaller version of a regimental cap badge added above it including the Essex and Middlesex Regiments and the King's Royal Rifle Corps.

N33

Keen to keep the spirit of the Home Guard alive and give members an opportunity to retain their ability to use firearms, the government encouraged the formation of Home Guard Rifle Clubs. Several produced lapel badges; examples noted include those for the Leek Home Guard and the 5th Sussex Home Guard Battalion in Worthing. Other units retained their connections though associations or Old Comrades clubs, many of which issued lapel badges.

P United against Axis tyranny: *Overseas Forces' Welfare*

The First Edition noted that the American Red Cross (ARC) in Great Britain issued a badge to British volunteers completing 150 hours work in their Service Clubs. Thanks to information supplied by the ARC's historian this is now known to be that with the blue background **(P10)**. The badge with a red background **(P11)** was awarded for three months volunteer work. London's largest ARC club was **Rainbow Corner** situated between Piccadilly Circus and Leicester Square. Non-uniformed staff there wore their own badge **(P13)**. In October 1943 the ARC's newspaper 'London Light' announced that a similar badge with a 'Boxing' bar below would be awarded to those winning bouts at the club. The earliest club for Americans in London, The Eagle in Charing Cross Road which opened in December 1940, was taken over by the ARC in April 1942. The badge worn by staff **(P14)** has rings below suggesting that bars could be attached to show the wearer's role or length

NEW AWARD FOR E.T.O. BOXERS

Instead of the *Star and Stripes* Bout Winner Belts which were awarded to winning boxers last season, the American Red Cross Athletic Department has devised a new award in the form of an enamelled red, white and blue medallion, with provision for an additional bar to be added for each successive bout won by the boxer.

The medallion is shown in the small photograph, and the winners in the first three Rainbow Corner cards were presented with the new award. Athletic Department officials are wondering who will be the first boxer to have the coveted bar added to his medal.

A.R.C. Photo

P13   P14   P15

of service. A badge **(P15)** was also worn by staff working at the **ARC Women's Service Club** in Charles Street, Mayfair, the majority British volunteers from Bermondsey.

Many American ARC staff worked on Clubmobiles, London Green Line buses converted to mobile canteens which taking hot coffee and fresh doughnuts to isolated American units such as the ground crews working on bomber airfields in East Anglia. Long term workers on these canteens were awarded the **"Distinguished Doughnut Cluster"**; hanging from a rectangular white metal brooch inscribed in red 'American Red Cross/Doughnut Cluster', a small, circular white enamel disc edged in blue was decorated with three donuts and a steaming cup of coffee. The English spelling of 'Doughnut' rather than the American 'Donut' suggests the badge was made in England.

Although never stationed in Britain, Chinese forces were at war with Japan from July 1937. In 1942 the Bishop of Hong Kong and South China arrived in Britain seeking funds to aid Chinese civilians suffering misery and starvation resulting from the war. Lady Isobel Cripps wife of the Lord Privy Seal, Sir Stafford Cripps launched a national appeal 'British United Aid to China' which raised nearly three million pounds. The funds, used to provide relief across China, were distributed by a committee headed by the British Ambassador, Sir Horace Seymour. A shield-shaped lapel badge with the fund's name surrounding the flag of the Nationalist Chinese is recorded.

Q Humanity keeps an appointment: *The Red Cross and St John's*

In August 1937 the St John Ambulance Brigade announced the creation of an ARP Auxiliary Reserve 'a body of men and women drawn from the general public, not being already members of the Brigade'.

Q13   Q14   Q15

Q16   Q17   Q18

Having attended the Brigade's ARP lectures and passed their examinations Volunteers agreed to maintain their knowledge of ARP work and perform ARP duties in wartime with their local unit or any other they preferred. A celluloid lapel badge **(Q13)** was issued to the Reserve's members.

The SJAB had a long history of forming units in industrial premises many of which expanded to create the industrial first aid parties formed under the terms of the Civil Defence Act. Where no parties existed the SJAB and the British Red Cross Society trained volunteers. Five examples of ARP badges used by industrial First Aid Parties are shown, the first **(Q14)**, for the Glasgow shipbuilders **Fairfields**, a variation on **C54**. On the river at Purfleet, Essex, **Thames Board Mills (Q15)** recruited 400 staff to its ARP organisation, 45 of them first aiders. The raids on the mills which killed twenty workers proved their worth. Rotherham's **Park Gate Iron & Steel Co Ltd** issued their First Aiders **(Q16)** with a variation of **C91**. **Rootes Securities (Q17)** continued manufacturing their Hillman and Commer vehicles and built aircraft. The **Peterborough Cooperative Society (Q18)** was one of many cooperatives providing services ranging from groceries to funerals in most British towns and cities.

R For Men on Active Service: *Service Welfare*

Badges for two further local comforts committees have been recorded since the First Edition, that for the City of Cardiff (**R33**) operating under the patronage of the Lady Mayoress. The **Highland War Comforts** badge (**R34**) is believed to have been formed from the Highland Societies which originated in the eighteenth century to foster interest in Highland customs and traditions.

Until rationing made wool hard to find the main activity of comfort funds was knitting scarves, pullovers, socks and gloves to supplement the clothing supplied to the armed forces. The Voluntary Knitter badge for **RAF Hemswell (R35)**, a Bomber Command station in Lincolnshire, was probably issued to those knitting for RAF Hemswell rather than RAF personnel on the station knitting in their spare time. Completed items were packed for delivery to the recipients, in the later war years usually the Red Cross; the Voluntary Packer badge from Nottinghamshire (**R36**) is a variation of R17. Other enamel

R33

R34

R35

R36

R37

R38

badges recorded were for The Bolton and District Comforts Fund, The Leeds Knitting Circle, The Tunbridge Wells Knitting Society and the St Andrew's Ambulance Association War Work Party. A 'Worker for Dorset Comforts 1939' celluloid badge also existed.

 A common welfare activity was the operation of canteens for servicemen and women in transit or stationed away from major centres. In Bury St Edmunds, Suffolk the Athenaeum, built as the town's assembly rooms in the eighteenth century, operated as a service club, its badge **(R37)** incorporating the 'VW' in 1940 for voluntary welfare workers not under the patronage of a local comforts committee. The All-Services Canteen in Poulton-Le-Fylde in Lancashire **(R38)** probably served a large number of airmen; taking advantage of the town's numerous boarding houses and hotels, the RAF's largest training base in Britain was based in nearby Blackpool. The POW Comforts Fund badge **(R29)** also exists with a Staffordshire knot at its centre.

S   Twice the number of human beings: *Animals at War*

Two further NARPAC badges can be added to those in the First Edition. **S9** is the same as **S3** but with a blue scroll instead of a white. The reason for the difference is unknown. A badge with a white scroll marked 'HQ Staff' has also been recorded. It is still not possible to identify all ten of the badges that a contemporary list says were issued by NARPAC.

S9

T John Bull pulls in his belt: *Food and Salvage*

The green Salvage Steward badge (T9) worn by full-time stewards in factories can now be illustrated. The 'Cog' badge for Junior Salvage Stewards **(L9)** has been recorded in gold

T9

T10

although whether this is a higher national award or a local variation given to more successful junior collectors is not know. A celluloid version has a blue cog on a red ground with 'A cog in the wheel' in white around the edge. A recorded celluloid badge has 'Rubber Salvage Commando' surrounding an image of a soldier brandishing a Thompson sub-machine gun. Apart from the badge worn by the Salvage Stewards in the City of Chester (**T10**) the only additional metal badge recorded originates in Lincolnshire; shield-shaped, this has a gold V for Victory at its centre surrounded by 'Louth Voluntary Salvage Worker'.

U Back the Great Attack: *The National Savings Movement*

As the First Edition noted the Spitfire Funds of 1940 were the earliest wartime savings campaign. Enamel badges for funds organised by Kidsgrove Urban District and Clifton Cinemas have been recorded. A blue enamel badge with 'Shareholder' under a Spitfire exists in two versions, one version 'Vauxhall-Bedford' on the reverse the second with 'Otley Motors' suggesting a motor industry fund. Two enamel badges, one circular the other oval, are simply marked 'Spitfire Fund'. Badges U8 and **U9** exist stamped 'City of Wells', Oldbury Women's' and 'Stourbridge'; a similar winged badge is stamped 'St Pancras Bomber Club'. In addition to the Finsbury badge (**U36**), celluloid Spitfire badges were issued by Buxton, Calne, Portslade and Redditch. A celluloid example from Cheadle may have been issued after the more elaborate metal version (**U12**). No badge has yet been found for the Hendon Fighter Fund.

U36

Shortages of materials meant that subsequent National Savings campaigns beginning with War Weapons Weeks between September 1940 and October 1941 produced only celluloid badges. Five of the nineteen additional War Weapons badges recorded feature warships, ten aircraft and three tanks; the nineteenth bears emblems of the three services. The design of badge **U16** was also issued by Halesowen and Tipton, **U17** by Ludlow and District and Wenlock, **U20** by Shepton Mallett. Badges for Warship Weeks in 1942 have been recorded for Accrington, Brentwood, Brighton, Canterbury, Castle Cary, Cheltenham, Dudley, Evesham, Farnham Royal, Halesowen, Helston, Malvern, Manchester, North Cotswold, Oldbury, Surbiton, Wenlock, Wolverhampton and Worcester. Those for Brentwood, Evesham, Malvern, Wenlock and Worcester are of the same design as **U27**. Three of these come from the same county, suggesting a degree of co-ordination between local Savings Committees. All of these badges are in the same format as **U14** to **U27** except for that of Farnham Royal which is of the same manufacture as the Wings for

TELEGRAMS:
"ENTHUSIASM,"
BIRMINGHAM.

THIS BUSINESS WAS FOUNDED IN 1827
AND THE WELL KNOWN THOMAS FATTORINI PRODUCTIONS HAVE (DURING
SEVEN REIGNS) BEEN MANUFACTURED CONTINUOUSLY IN THIS COUNTRY
BY SUCCESSIVE GENERATIONS OF THE FATTORINI FAMILY.

TELEPHONE:
CENTRAL 1307-8
BIRMINGHAM.

THOMAS FATTORINI LTD.

REGENT STREET WORKS
BIRMINGHAM 1

MANUFACTURING
GOLDSMITHS AND
SILVERSMITHS

ARTICLES BEARING OUR
NAME OR INITIALS ARE
FULLY GUARANTEED

CONTRACTORS TO HIS MAJESTY'S GOVERNMENT

MEDALS - BADGES - CUPS - SHIELDS - TROPHIES - CASKETS - REGALIA

IN REPLY PLEASE QUOTE OUR REF. **WW/BU.**   YOUR REF.   **26th August, 1941.**

To National Savings Committees of
Mayors & Lord Mayors

Dear Sir,   Re "Warships Week".   *WW/BU Env. (498*

       With reference to the recent Broadcast and Press
Notices concerning the above, may we once again stress the
advantages to be gained by the adoption of a nicely designed
Badge for the supporters of your local "Warship Week".

       We were privileged to make many tens of thousands
of Badges for the numerous "War Weapons Weeks" held all over
the United Kingdom during the last twelve months, and wherever
the Badges were used, we heard of their great success.   They
quickened local interest, gave daily and widespread publicity
to an ever increasing circle, and gained much increased support
to the Appeals as a result.

       Very often, the demand far exceeded the numbers purchased
by our customers, and the proceeds from the sales provided a
very gratifying margin to cover the incidentals of the Appeals
concerned.

       If you are interested in this matter, we shall be happy
to submit designs, samples and suggestions, entirely without
obligation, and the keenest possible estimate submitted on
receipt of particulars of the quantity likely to be required.

       We hope to be able to help you make your "Warship Week"
a big success.

            Yours faithfully,
             for THOMAS FATTORINI LTD.

LOOK FOR THOMAS IN OUR NAME AS SIMILAR FIRMS ARE NOT THE SAME

Victory badges **U28** to **U30**. A 'Wings' badge identical in design to U30 has been noted for Torquay. Only the designs shown as **U31** and **U34** appear to have been used for Salute the Soldier Weeks; **U34** has been recorded for Oldbury and Exeter, **U31** for Axminster, Barnstaple, Gloucester, North Cotswolds, Ottery St Mary, Rugby, Sherborne, Stratford-upon-Avon and Tewkesbury.

Like many other badges illustrated in the book a large number of the celluloid National Savings campaign badges were manufactured in Birmingham by Thomas Fattorini Ltd. Their letter claims they made 'tens of thousands' for War Weapons Weeks and were aiming to do the same for Warship Weeks; the ink annotation shows it was sent to nearly 500 organising committees.

V18   V19

V Sing with ENSA!: *Entertaining and the Media*

Badge **V17** has still not been positively connected with the Home Front in Britain but it does have a connection with the Home Front in India where it was worn by the uniformed staff of the Civil Censorship Office. The author would be interested to learn of any evidence of a connection with British censorship.

Despite their efforts ENSA alone could not provide sufficient entertainment for all the troops stationed in Britain. From the first days of the war their efforts were supplemented by local amateur performers, although their normal jobs and lack of transport meant they were not always available when needed and their standard was very variable.

The army's Northern Command formed an Association of Artistes for Entertaining the Troops which ran 15 concert parties and two choirs as their **Voluntary Entertainment Service** under the auspices of the Command's Army Welfare Services. Members wore a VES badge **(V18)**.

Britain's newspapers played an essential part in the war effort. Like most major industrial concerns, Kemsley House in London's Gray's Inn Road, home to the Daily Sketch and Sunday Graphic, had its own ARP staff. This version of their ARP badge **(V19)** has an unusual extra bar indicating that the wearer was a member of Kemsley's ARP Committee.

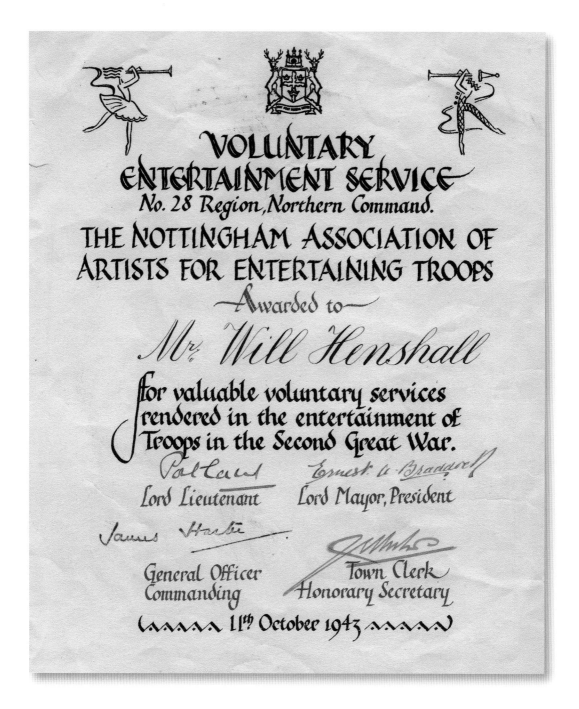

VOLUNTARY ENTERTAINMENT SERVICE
No. 28 Region, Northern Command.
THE NOTTINGHAM ASSOCIATION OF ARTISTS FOR ENTERTAINING TROOPS
Awarded to
Mr Will Henshall
for valuable voluntary services rendered in the entertainment of Troops in the Second Great War.

Lord Lieutenant   Lord Mayor, President

General Officer Commanding   Town Clerk Honorary Secretary

11th October 1943

W Lend a hand on the Land: *The Agricultural War Effort*

With the import of food from overseas restricted from the first day of the war Britain's farms were vitally important to the war effort. Ensuring that they were working to maximum capacity were 61 County War Agricultural Executive Committees controlled by the Ministry of Agriculture and Fisheries. The War Ags' were made up of farmers, landowners, workers' representatives and local bodies or individuals concerned with food

W10   W11   W12

W13   W14   W15

production. War Ags had powers to direct the cultivation of underused or neglected land and under certain circumstances could confiscate a farmer's land to ensure its productive use. The Devon Committee War Ag badge **(W10)** is the only one yet recorded. Agricultural labour was a constant headache despite the activities of the Women's Land Army and the numerous Italian Prisoners of War who arrived from the Middle East from 1941 to work on Britain's farms. Volunteers recruited to help with annual harvests were variously described as Emergency Land Workers **(W11)**, Emergency Land Corps **(W12)** or Auxiliary Land Corps, these workers often all women. Scarcity of materials meant that many of the badges issued to these volunteers were celluloid with tin backs. Warwickshire's badge **(W12)** is identical in style to **W9**.

Even this augmented agricultural labour force could not produce enough food. In October 1939 the Minister of Agriculture launched 'Dig for Victory' campaign to cultivate half a million new allotments, the campaign's shovel and boot **(W13)** effective reminders of what was required. With magazines and books deluging gardeners with advice on becoming self-sufficient, at the beginning of 1940 **The National Garden Club (W14)** was formed 'by a few enthusiastic horticulturalists' to provide advice to those gardening for the first time. Members received a magazine and a series of seasonal bulletins with the added of the NGC's offer to supply vegetable seeds of guaranteed quality to members. The results achieved by the gardeners who dug for victory went on display at local exhibitions such as that held in Bolton in September 1942 **(W15)**.

X Citizenship through training: *Youth Organisations*

When the National Association of Girls Training Corps was formed in March 1942 membership of the various girls training corps was restricted to girls aged 16 to 18. Those under 16 already members could no longer serve. The **Junior Girls Training Corps** was formed in July 1943 for girls between 14 and 16, the first company in Doncaster that September. Two JGTC badges, the existence of which was suggested in the First Edition are shown; in white metal for girls **(X19)**, red enamel **(X20)** for officers.

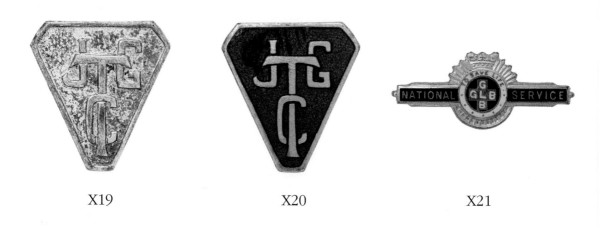

X19   X20   X21

X22   X23

Prior to the Second World War the main youth organisations for girls were the Brownies and Girl Guides, the latter wearing a cloth War Service badge on their uniform in place of a metal badge. Although a much smaller organisation, The Girls Life Brigade claimed to be the oldest uniformed organisation for girls having been formed in 1902 by the National Sunday School Union as an interdenominational Christian organisation. By 1943 the GLB had over 40,000 members and claimed in a magazine article that year that 'GLB members practised signalling … long before the women's auxiliary services were thought of'. Their wartime activities were similar to those of all youth organisations in wartime. It is not known how GLB members qualified for their National Service badge **(X21)**.

Before the creation of the pre-service corps several local authorities sought to involve young people not already members of organisations like the Scouts and Guides in working for the war effort. In July 1940 East Suffolk County Council appealed to young people to 'get together to form a Youth Squad to do work of national importance'. Within three months the county had 1.450 members in 142 Youth Squads. Similar initiatives were the Bolton Youth Service Corps and Hertfordshire's Youth Service Squads. Officially encouraged by the Board of Education from March 1941, their activities were eclipsed later that year by the formation of Girls Training Corps and government support for the SCC, ACF, ATC whose uniforms were a more visible sign of National Service than lapel badges **(X22-X23)** worn by Youth Squads and Corps. In May 1941 Girl Guides were told they could wear Youth Service Corps badges on their uniforms. It is not known how many Corps or Squads existed.

Y Is your journey really necessary?: *The Transport Industry*

All forms of transport were vital to the war effort. The 'Big Four' railway companies were placed under government control through the Railway Executive Committee (REC) which worked alongside the **Railway Clearing House (Y13)** to ensure a fair distribution of the shared income to railway companies. No examples of the badges issued by the light railway companies also controlled by the REC and listed in the First Edition have yet been seen.

Although no specific badges for Air Raid Precautions duties on the 'Big Four' have yet been recorded ARP was as vital to the railways as to any other company. The badge for Ireland's **Great Northern Railway (GNR)** is unusual. GNR main line services ran from Belfast to Dublin, a route complicated by the border between Northern and Southern Ireland which crossed it. As Ireland remained neutral it seems likely that the badge **(Y14)**

Y13

Y14

Y15

Y16

Y17

Y18

Y19

was only worn in Northern Ireland where blackout and the ARP measures applied as in the rest of the United Kingdom. Their services were doubtless appreciated when Belfast suffered air raids in April and May 1941.

Transporting goods from Britain's docks and harbours remained a major activity for the railways. As activity at Britain's southern and eastern coastal ports declined, west coast ports made a major contribution to the war effort. One of the largest was Liverpool run under the auspices of the Ministry of War Transport by the **Mersey Docks and Harbour Board (Y15)**. Home to the Atlantic convoys and their Royal Navy escorts the port suffered 68 air attacks between 1940 and 1941 but passed 75 million tons of cargo and nearly five million troops conveyed in 1,285 convoys in the war years.

The many private canals between London and Birmingham finally came under the control of one company in the 1930s making it possible for **The Grand Union Canal Carrying Company Co Ltd (Y16)** founded in 1934 to transport freight easily between the two cities. Traffic declined in wartime partly due to the loss of men to the armed forces, their place taken by women volunteers who became known as 'Idle Women' from the blue plastic National Service badge they wore **(Y17)**. The GUCC came under the control of the Ministry of War Transport in 1942. Its assets were taken over by the nationalised British Transport Commission in 1949.

The **River Emergency Service** formed by the Port of London Authority as a uniformed civil defence force on the River Thames which was referred to in the First Edition issued the lapel badge illustrated **(Y18)**.

Private motoring gradually declined as the war effort claimed petrol and rubber but not before a local initiative in Birmingham produced the badge of the **VTS (Y19)**. Just before Christmas 1939 a group of business men meeting in a city hotel learned of the service men and women on leave stranded at railway stations all night without transport to get them home. Five car owners visited New Street Station that night and carried 40 passengers home. By March 1940 130 regular volunteers had formed the Voluntary Transport Service, displaying VTS on their badge and the windscreens of their cars. Petrol rationing brought an end to the service in January 1943 when they had carried 95,000 passengers. Restarted in January 1945 the VTS continued to operate until June 1946.

Carrying On

Appendix

The WVS at War : the work of the Women's Voluntary Services in 1943.

The list reproduced below was compiled in June 1943 for The Committee on Honours and Awards in Wartime when the WVS were being considered for the issue of war service chevrons. It illustrates the wide variety of tasks carried out by this essential wartime organisation and the numbers employed for these duties.

	Role	Numbers employed
1)	**Organisation**	
	Central Executive Staff	6,194
	Office Staff	4,106
	Local Representatives	31,559
2)	**Billeting and Welfare**	
	Billeting	11,682
	General welfare	10,055
	Wartime nurseries for under 5s	1,584
	Clothing for those rendered homeless	8,926
3)	**ARP**	
	Wardens	4,114
	FAP, Gas cleansing etc.	23,390
	Report Centres	6,557
	Ambulances	40,030
	Reinforcement Bases	2,411
4)	**Housewives Service**	264,899
5)	**Homeless Services**	
	Rest Centres	173,053
	Information Bureaux	4,424
	Mobile Teams	4,979
6)	**Food Services**	
	British Restaurants	10,511
	School Meals	1,898

	Rural Feeding Scheme	963
	Queens Messengers and Emergency	
	Mobile Canteens	10,071
	Civil Defence Canteens	7,960
	Static Emergency Feeding	18,760
7)	**Work For HM Forces**	
	Static Canteens, Hostels and Clubs	27,253
	Mobile Troop Canteens	879
	Camouflage	Not known
	Home Guard	8,237
	Others	1,936
8)	**Hospital Workers**	6,716
9)	**Work Party Members**	26,130
10)	**Transport**	
	Drivers	5,894
	Messengers	2,868
11)	**Salvage**	Not known
12)	**National Savings**	5,350
13)	**Other Activities**	
	Clerical	6,860
	Miscellaneous	15,041
	Total enrolled membership	966,425

Select Bibliography

The items listed, both published and unpublished, represent a selection of the sources used in the compilation of this book. The scarcity of information on many of the organisations recorded means that details have been collated from numerous sources, not all of which appear in this list.

Published Sources

ACF Association	*The Army Cadet Force Handbook* (The Association, 1967)
Bookbinder, P	*Marks & Spencer : the war years, 1939-1945* (Century Benham, 1989)
Briggs, S	*Those Radio Times* (Weidenfeld & Nicolson, 1981)
Cambray, P G	*The Red Cross and St John War Organisation 1939-1947* (BRCS, 1949)
Central Statistical Office	*Statistical digest of the War* (HMSO, 1951)
Critchley, T	*History of the Police in England and Wales 900-1966* (Constable, 1967)
Dean, B	*Theatre at War* (Harrap, 1956)
Dunn, C L	*Emergency Medical Services* (HMSO, 1952)
Froggatt, D J	*Railway buttons, badges and uniforms* (Ian Allan, 1986)
Graves, Charles	*Women in Green* (Heinemann, 1948)
Hammerton, J (Ed)	*History of the Second Great War* (Amalgamated Press, nd)
Home Office and Home Security, Ministry of	*Circulars 1937-1945* (HMSO, 1937-1945)

Le Marec, Bernard   *Les Francais Libres et leurs emblemes* (Lauvauzelle et Cie, 1964)

Longmate, N   *How we lived then* (Hutchinson, 1971)

MacInnes, C M   *Bristol at War* (Museum Press, 1962)

Mills, Jon   *A People's Army* (Wardens Publishing, 1994)

Newman Books   *Municipal Yearbook 1940* (Newman, 1940)

O'Brien, Terence   *Civil Defence* (HMSO, 1955)

Pratt Insh, G   *The wartime history of the Scottish Branch of the British Red Cross Society* (Jackson, 1952)

RAF Comforts Committee   *Farewell Berkeley Square; a survey of the work of the Committee 1939-1946* (The Committee, 1946)

St Hill Bourne, D   *They Also Serve* (Winchester Publishing, 1947)

Stacey, C P   *The Half-million: The Canadians in Britain 1939-1946* (University of Toronto Press, 1987)

Thomas, N and McCouaig, S   *Foreign Volunteers of the Allied Forces 1939-1945* (Osprey, 1991)

Tilling, Thomas & Co.   *The War that Went on Wheels* (Tilling, 1947)

Times Newspaper   *British War Production 1939-1945* (Times, 1946)

Titmus, R M   *Problems of Social Policy* (HMSO, 1950)

War Office   *Army Welfare* (War Office, 1953)

Whittaker, Len   *Stand Down* (R Westlake Books, 1990)

Winslow, T E   *Forewarned is forearmed* (Hodge & Co., 1948)

Periodicals

Issues of the following magazines for the wartime period :

ATC Gazette, Picture Post, PLA Monthly, Scouter Magazine, Sea Cadet, War Illustrated

Unpublished Sources

The records of the London County Council in the Greater London Record Office.

The files of the War Office and the Ministries of Home Security and Health in the Public Record Office, Kew.

The archives of the following organisations:

> The London Boroughs of Camden, Lambeth, Southwark, Wandsworth and Westminster and the Corporation of the City of London.
> Glasgow City Council.
> The London Fire Brigade.
> The National Council of YMCAs.
> The Post Office.
> The Women's Voluntary Services.

In early 1940 it was suggested that a badge should be designed for those invalided out of the forces due to injuries sustained on active service. A primary requirement was that it should be easily distinguishable from the First World War pattern. It was also felt that the use of the words "For King and Empire", which had appeared on the earlier badge were not appropriate as the new conflict was not seen as an Empire war. At the suggestion of the King's Private Secretary, Sir Alexander Hardinge, the words "For Loyal Sevice" were used instead. A design by the sculptor Mr Percy Metcalfe was agreed upon in November 1940, although an announcement of the existence of the badge was delayed until stocks were ready.

The eventual design was solid with the agreed wording around the edge of a circle at the centre of which were the Royal cypher "GRI" and the crown. The majority of badges were made with lapel fixings, but a much smaller quantity with a brooch fitting was made for women. It was manufactured by civilian firms in German silver, not sterling as had been the First World War issue. Smaller commercial versions also exist.

The badge was issued to all those invalided out of the services through pensionable war injury. In addition to members of the Army, Navy and RAF, it was also awarded to the Merchant Navy, Fishing Fleets, the Pilotage and Light Vessel Services and Naval Auxiliary personnel. A suggestion that its use be extended to the Civil Defence Services was turned down. Announced in the press in May 1941, initial issue of the badge began in November. The scheme was administered by the Ministry of Pensions, each badge being dispatched by registered post in a small cardboard box with a forwarding letter, at the bottom of which was a tear-off receipt.

Index

Company names, organisations and place names mentioned in the text are listed below. Both abbreviations and full titles are included as initials are often the only identifying feature on many of these badges. Badge illustrations are indexed only when they are **not** referred to in the text.

Index

Index

Index